FOR KING & EMPIRE

THE CANADIANS AT AMIENS

August 8th to 16th, 1918

A Social History and Battlefield Tour

by N. M. Christie

For King & Empire; Volume VII

CEF BOOKS

1999

© NORM CHRISTIE 1999

Canadian Cataloguing in Publication Data
Christie, N.M.
The Canadians at Amiens, August, 1918
(For King & Empire; 7)
Includes bibliographical references.

ISBN 1-896979-20-3

1. Amiens, Battle of, 1918. 2. World War, 1914-18--Campaigns--France.
3.Canada. Canadian Army--History--World War, 1914-1918. I. Title. II. Series:
Christie, N.M. For King & Empire: 7.

D545.A56C48   1998940.4'35   C98-900897-5

Publication of this book has been supported
by the Canadian War Museum.

Published by: CEF BOOKS
                         P.O. Box 40083
                         2440 Bank Street
                         Ottawa, Ontario, K1V 0W8

Other books in this Series

Also by CEF BOOKS:

Ghosts Have Warm Hands by Will R. Bird
Letters of Agar Adamson edited by N.M. Christie
The Journal of Private Fraser edited by R.H. Roy
For Freedom and Honour? by A.B. Godefroy

Front cover: Demuin British Cemetery, France. Photograph by N. Christie.

Printed in Canada

TABLE OF CONTENTS

KEEP YOUR MOUTH SHUT!

The success of any operation we carry out depends chiefly on surprise.

DO NOT TALK.—When you know that your Unit is making preparations for an attack, don't talk about them to men in other Units or to strangers, and keep your mouth shut, especially in public places.

Do not be inquisitive about what other Units are doing; if you hear or see anything, keep it to yourself.

If you hear anyone else talking about operations, stop him at once.

The success of the operations and the lives of your comrades depend upon your SILENCE.

If you ever should have the misfortune to be taken prisoner, don't give the enemy any information beyond your rank and name. In answer to all other questions you need only say, " I cannot answer."

He cannot compel you to give any other information. He may use threats. He will respect you if your courage, patriotism, and self-control do not fail. Every word you say may cause the death of one of your comrades.

Either after or before you are openly examined, Germans, disguised as British Officers or men, will be sent among you or will await you in the cages or quarters or hospital to which you are taken.

Germans will be placed where they can overhear what you say without being seen by you.

DO NOT BE TAKEN IN BY ANY OF THESE TRICKS.

Ptd. in France by A.P. & S.S. Press C. X477. 500000. 7/18.

This "notice" was posted into the Pay Book of every Canadian Soldier prior to the Amiens move.

INTRODUCTION TO THE BATTLE OF AMIENS
August 8th-16th 1918

August 8th 1918, the opening day of the Battle of Amiens, became known as "The Black Day." But for the first time in the war it was "The Black Day" for the German Army. The Canadians and Australians, attacking side-by-side, smashed the Germans at Amiens and drove them back 13 km capturing 12,000 prisoners and 2,000 machine-guns. It was a crushing victory and one that turned the tide on the Western Front in the First World War.

For the Canadians the attack was a tremendous achievement. They had only arrived at the front the previous week. Their move to the Amiens sector from the north had been in complete secrecy, for the Germans knew the Canadian Corps was well rested and at full strength. Any indication of their presence would have implied an imminent attack and eliminated the element of surprise. And with little time to reconnoitre the positions they were to attack, Amiens was to be the ultimate test for the Canadians. The record of victories in 1917; at Vimy, Arleux, Fresnoy, Hill 70 and Passchendaele had produced an attitude of unbridled confidence within the Corps. August 8th was to challenge the planning, efficiency and courage of all their men from the Generals in Headquarters to the Privates in the field.

There was more than just pride driving the Canadians at Amiens, there was also revenge. In June 1918, a German U-Boat, U-86, torpedoed a Canadian Hospital Ship. There were 94 Canadian Army Medical Corps personnel on board, including 14 Canadian Nursing Sisters. In the ensuing exodus from the sinking H.S. Llandovery Castle, all Canadian Medical staff made their escape to the lifeboats. In an act of barbarity, the U-Boat Captain ordered the survivors machine-gunned. The 14 Canadian Nursing Sisters perished as their lifeboat vanished into the sucking vortex of the sinking ship. Eighty-eight of the 94 Canadians drowned. The newspapers and the propaganda machine played up the atrocity so by August 1918, the Amiens operation was code-named "Llandovery Castle", and revenge was in the mind of the attacking Canadians, and it was revenge they got.

The tremendous success of the first day was followed up by another great advance on August 9th. In the ensuing days more German reinforcements arrived and the battle ground to a halt, and finally by August 12th, was called off.

The Canadian losses for the Battle of Amiens were 11,362 dead, wounded and missing. They had advanced 22 km, captured 9,000 Germans, 190 guns and more than 1,000 machine-guns, and had avenged the Llandovery Castle.

There was little time for the Canadians to celebrate. By August 20th they were on the move to Arras and on August 26th they launched their greatest attack of the war. Between August 26th and September 5th, the Canadians suffered a further 9,000 casualties. Never out of the line, the Canadian Corps launched the next major attack on September 27th, 1918. It was their third major offensive in 50 days! This time the objective was Cambrai. After heavy fighting Cambrai fell and the Canadian Corps pursued the Germans until the war ended at Mons, November 11th, 1918.

The three major attacks at Amiens, Arras and Cambrai, cost the Canadian Corps a shocking 46,405 casualties, including 11,882 dead.

The Road to Victory started on that misty morning in front of Amiens, August 8th, 1918. Attacking in waves, and supported by tanks and cavalry, the men swept over the Somme farmland and proved the Germans could be beaten. It was a brilliant victory.

The quiet countryside of the Santerre plain and the Luce river valley, east of Amiens, is still as it was 80 years ago. The village church towers are visible today as they were on that misty morning. Gone are the guns and wire and all that remains are the small cemeteries containing the Canadian dead. These sleepy places keep alive the memory of those courageous Canadians; those men who made "The Black Day".

ABOUT ARRAS

To be consistent with the other books in this series, this book recommends Arras as your centre of operations for visiting the Amiens battlefield, which is 50 kilometres south. Other Canadian battlefields; Vimy 1917, Arras 1918, Cambrai 1918 and the Somme 1916 are within 30 km of Arras. However Amiens is also a great place to centre your tour for the Battles of Amiens and the Somme (see About Amiens). Virtually everything that can be said about Arras can be said about Amiens, the capital of the Somme.

Of Roman origin, Arras was a stronghold in Julius Caesar's day. It was originally built on Baudimont Hill, east of the Crinchon Stream which runs through the town and called Atrebatum after a tribe which lived in the area, the Atrebates. Arras is a corruption of that name.

In the 5th century, during the reign of the Frankish king, Clovis I, Christianity was preached by Saint-Vaast, who created the diocese of Arras and was its first bishop. The most important abbey in the region was built in the 600s to honour the saint. A new town gradually emerged under the protection of this powerful monastery and eventually separated from the original construction by a continuous line of fortifications. By the 11th century, the two communities were quite independent of each other, each with its own form of government. The older Roman city on Baudimont Hill was the Cité of Arras and was under the jurisdiction of the bishop. The other, to the west, was the Ville proper and a dependency of the St. Vaast Abbey.

While the Ville grew steadily, the Cité gradually declined until the mid-18th century when it was incorporated in the Ville. Until Arras became part of the kingdom in France in the mid-17th century, the "Ville", as the capital of the County of Artois, successively belonged to the Counts of Flanders (850-1180), to the Counts of Artois (1180-1384), to the Dukes of Burgundy (1384-1492) and finally to the Kings of Spain (1492-1640).

The French kings often interfered in the affairs of Arras throughout this period. The town was besieged four times by the kings of France in the 9th and 10th centuries. In the 14th century,

Arras was torn by popular sedition. Under the Dukes of Burgundy, and especially under Philippe-le-Bon, the town's world-renowned cloth and tapestry industries enjoyed a period of great prosperity. Its Arrazi tapestries became famous.

Arras is also infamous for imprisoning Joan of Arc during October and November 1430.

When Louis XI tried to claim Artois in 1477, the Cité of Arras promptly opened its gates to the Royal Army, but the Ville refused to surrender and was only conquered in 1479, after a long siege. Furious at the people's resistance, Louis XI exiled all the inhabitants and brought in the "Ligeriens." Arras became Spanish and its name was changed to Franchise. A few months later, the people of Arras were allowed to return to their homes, and in 1483, its ancient name, armorial bearings and laws were restored.

The inhabitants of Arras resisted French domination for years following the incident with Louis XI. They opened their gates to the German and Burgundian troops of Austria in 1492, only to regret doing so when the Germans pillaged and rifled their valuables.

The Spanish-controlled city again came under the rule of the kings of France in the mid-17th century, when it fell after a long and bloody siege. The bombardments caused great damage to the abbey. A decade or so later, the town held out heroically against a Spanish invasion for 45 days.

Birth place of Augustin Robespierre, Arras was not spared during the Revolution. In 1793, Joseph Le Bon, sent there on a mission, organized the Terror. The guillotine was permanently erected in the Place de la Comédie. Travellers avoided Arras and the local merchants stopped doing business.

During the Great War, the Germans occupied Arras for only three days, September 6-9, 1914. But after their departure, the "Martyrdom of Arras" began. The Germans remained at the gates of the city until April 1917. Bombardment began October 6, 1914. Gunners fired ceaselessly on the military quarters and the two famous squares. The Hôtel de Ville, the Abbey of Saint Vaast and the Cathedral were burnt down, the belfry destroyed and by April 1917, Arras was completely in ruins. In March 1918, when the great German Offensive began, the bombardments broke out afresh, inhabitants were evacuated and by the end of August, the British drove the enemy out for good.

A visit to Arras should begin in the architecturally-unique Grand'Place, once an orchard belonging to the Abbey of Saint Vaast, and the Petite-Place. These squares have been bordered with gabled private houses and edged with stone columns and elliptical arches supporting vaulted galleries for hundreds of years.

Merchants once drew crowds of buyers to their stalls under the porticos of the squares and the famous tapestries of Arras were once made in the damp cellars under the galleries.

A bunch of Canadians in Arras. February, 1918

Arras, March 1918.

There are places in the world that are holy because in the long unwinding of the thread of time no human foot has trod there, and they have never had any part in the confused stretch and strain which we, more than the animals and the plants, cast about our living. And there are places in the world that are holy because for centuries and centuries they have been witnesses of unconscious participants in, that very stretch and strain. Arras is one of these. The wanderer through the crooked streets of Arras may set his foot upon soil that was used to the goings and the comings of man when Nero was emperor in Rome, and for centuries before. Arras has been the centre of a diocese, and the place of residence of a bishop, since the fourth century. The Netherlanders have possessed this soil, and the Austrians and the Spanish and the French. It has been burned over, pillaged, drenched in blood, times without number. One cannot visit Arras at any time without hearing in one's ears the call of the past. And how much more that morning when I entered her for the first time, to find an Arras in the very clutch of disaster, deserted by her people, the enemy at her eastern gate! Far more vividly than if the good citizens of 1918 had been there, stamping with their talk, their dress, their manners, the *Anno domini MCMXVIII* on everything in sight, the past seemed to arise and live again, and there was no jarring note. The civilians had been ordered to evacuate a day or so before, and nearly all had obeyed. As we rode slowly through the narrow, curving streets, between high walls of masonry, it was only at long intervals that the glimpse of a face from behind closed shop-shutters or a fleeting form disappearing around a corner, told us that human beings still lived there. Of the civilians we saw, most were women. A few soldiers were to be seen, but very few; the whole atmosphere of the city was emptiness. A place to dream. In fancy I peopled these quaint byways with characters out of fiction and history. I saw Jean Valjean hurrying to the court house to surrender himself, the shade of the young lawyer Robespierre stepped briskly along beside me, and at the ale-house on the corner I could hear the voice of brother Jerome Coignard spilling spicy philosophies into the ears of young Jacques Tournebroche.

Imagine a great city, now dead, which throbbed as late as yesterday with life. You traverse a narrow, circling way, high built on either side with stately fronts of stone and brick. The clatter of the horses' feet raises echoes which give back and forth a dozen times and die away to nothing among the corners of the walls. Inside the windows, in many cases, everything is left as it was when the panic-stricken populace (a city populace and less stable than the peasantry) fled away at the approach of the guns. The little shop-signs *Tobac, Coiffeur, Boulanger,* invite you to enter and buy; but the doors of the shops are fast barred. You pass some municipal building, courthouse perhaps, or *Mairie,* its stone facade plastered with *affiches* in gaudy red and blue. Church and theatre alike are silent, gloomy, mysterious. Only occasionally do you remark the destructive work of a shell disclosing the inner sacredness of a dwelling. And in the street lie the bodies of some horses, fresh killed. The Y.M.C.A. sign at the mouth of an abri is a familiar note; one spot at least in Arras had not been abandoned.

> *"When the sea, so deep and wide,*
> *Is frozen at Midsummer-tide,*
> *Then all upon the ice you'll see*
> *The Arras men their town shall flee."*

No such wonder had in fact taken place as the old catch prophesied, but surely greater wonders were recorded daily that year, wonders undreamed of by the poet who could imagine an ocean congealed in August.

James H. Pedley, MC, Lieutenant, 4th Canadian Infantry Battalion. From his memoir, *Only This.*

General Mewburn, Canadian Minister of Militia, visiting Arras. February 1918.

(PUBLIC ARCHIVES OF CANADA PA-3696)

Bordering the west side of the Petite-Place is the Hôtel de Ville, above which rises the graceful silhouette of the belfry. Long the centre of town, the Petite-Place attracted the townspeople to public meetings, festivals and public executions.

Today, the tourist office is located at the Hôtel de Ville (21 51 26 95) and is open daily. From there, guided tours can be arranged of the underground tunnels beneath the town hall (35 minutes, year-round). First used as cellars, the tunnels often served as shelters for the population during invasions and for the soldiers of the First World War. You can also visit the belfry.

Two-hour tours of the town are also offered by guide-lecturers of the National Association for Historical Sites and Buildings daily in July and August at 3:00 p.m. and Wednesdays and Saturdays in June and September at 3:00 p.m. Reserve at the tourist office.

The Abbey of Saint-Vaast shelters the rich collections of the Museum, and is a masterpiece of classical religious architecture.

Note, most museums in France are open 10:00 a.m. to noon and 2:00 to 6:00 p.m. and closed on Tuesdays. Sunday and winter hours may be reduced. Abbey tel. 21 71 26 43.

Arras is famous for its "cobalt blue" porcelain, first produced in the late 18th century. It is available in most tourist shops in the town centre.

Accommodation is not a problem in Arras. You may want to check out the following hotels:

Astoria, 10 place Foch, 62000 Arras, tel. 21 71 08 14

Hôtel Ibis, place Viviani, 62000 Arras, tel. 21 23 61 61

Mercure Hôtel (3-star), 58 boulevard Carnot, 62000 Arras, tel. 21 23 88 88

Hôtel Moderne, 1 boulevard Faidherbe, 62000 Arras, tel. 21 23 39 57

Ostel des 3 Luppars, 47 Grand'Place, 62000 Arras, tel. 21 07 41 41

Hôtel de l'Univers, 5 place Croix Rouge, 62000 Arras, tel. 21 71 34 01

Some eating establishments to consider are the restaurant at the Astoria which serves traditional French cuisine, tel. 21 71 29 78;

or *La Faisanderie*, 45 Grand'Place (opposite 3 Luppars), tel. 21 48 20 76. As well, there is a variety of restaurants and cafés at the station square.

ABOUT AMIENS

Amiens is the capital of the Department of the Somme and has a population of more than 130,000. It is on the major rail line running from Calais, and links with the Calais-Lille-Paris line (TGV) at Roye. It is 64 km south-west of Arras, 110 km north of Paris, and 110 km south-west of Lille.

Like all cities in France it has a rich history, full of conflict and invasions. Amiens places its origins to 54 BC, when Julius Caesar's Roman Legions set up camp at Samarobriva, and spent a long winter there encamped astride the Somme river. By 340 AD the name of the encampment was changed to Ambiens and later to Amiens. During the 5th to 8th centuries war scarred the Amienois countryside as it was invaded by the Franks and later by the Normans. The wars brought devastation to the region.

Always rich in architecture during the 12th and 13th centuries the Beffroi was built and construction was started on the Amiens Cathedral of Notre Dame. Being so close to the English Channel, Amiens was caught in The Hundred Years War, and to make matters worse suffered through a series of plagues. It was not until the 16th century that true economic prosperity was know and Amiens developed a rich garment industry. But even that could not stop the invasions and the Spaniards occupied the city and built the great Citadel in 1597. Throughout the next centuries, through the French Revolution, and the Napoleonic Wars, Amiens developed into the beautiful city it is today. Its old town quarter, Saint-Leu, became known as the Little Venice of the North, because of its canal system.

In the First World War Amiens was an important transport and supply centre. It was also an attractive location for officers and soldiers on leave. It luckily escaped with light destruction through the war until March 1918 when the Germans came within 10 km of capturing the city. Even with the Germans on the doorstep Amiens was not seriously damaged.

In the Second World War Amiens missed some of the heavy fighting during the Fall of France in 1940, but was damaged by Allied bombing raids, particularly in 1944. One of the most daring and certainly the most precise air raid of the war took place on February 18th, 1944, when British and New Zealander Mosquitoes bombed Amiens Prison with the objective of freeing imprisoned French Resistance fighters. The raid was successful and freed 50 of the Gestapo's doomed prisoners. Unfortunately 96 others were killed. The Group Leader's Mosquito was shot down and both crewmen were killed. P.C. Packard and J.A. Broadley are buried in St. Pierre Cemetery, Amiens, on the road to Albert, and just beside the Amiens Prison.

There is much to see in Amiens and a visit to the tourist office at bis 6, rue Duseval (tel. 03 22 71 60 50) will give you the information you will need to enjoy your time there.

There are numerous hotels and I have listed a few below:

Le Carlton, 42 rue de Noyon, 80000 Amiens,
tel. 03.22.97.72.22.

Novatel, CD 934 Longeau, 80440 Boves, tel. 03.22.46.22.22.

Ibis, 4, rur du Mal de Lattre de Tassigny, 80000 Amiens,
tel. 03.22.92.57.33.

Grand Hotel de líUnivers, 2, rue de Noyon, 80000 Amiens,
tel. 03.22.91.52.51.

Le Postillon, 17, place au Feurre, 80000 Amiens,
tel. 03.22.91.46.17.

La Ferme du Bois Gallant, CD 929, Querrieu,
tel. 03.22.40.13.42.

There are a large number of excellent restaurants in the old city, and the surrounding villages. There are even three McDonald's in Amiens for those with less adventurous palates. Remember, lunch is noon to 2 pm and dinner, after 7 pm.

COMPONENTS OF THE CANADIAN EXPEDITIONARY FORCE

AMIENS 1918

1ST CANADIAN DIVISION

1st Infantry Brigade	2nd Infantry Brigade	3rd Infantry Brigade
1st Battalion (Western Ontario)	5th Battalion (Saskatchewan)	13th Battalion (Black Watch of Montreal)
2nd Battalion (Eastern Ontario)	7th Battalion (British Columbia)	14th Battalion (Royal Montreal Regiment)
3rd Battalion (Toronto Regiment)	8th Battalion (90th Rifles of Winnipeg)	15th Battalion (48th Highlanders of Toronto)
4th Battalion (Central Ontario)	10th Battalion (Alberta)	16th Battalion (Canadian Scottish)

2ND CANADIAN DIVISION

4th Infantry Brigade	5th Infantry Brigade	6th Infantry Brigade
18th Battalion (Western Ontario)	22nd Battalion (Canadien-français)	27th Battalion (City of Winnipeg)
19th Battalion (Central Ontario)	24th Battalion (Victoria Rifles of Montreal)	28th Battalion (Saskatchewan)
20th Battalion (Central Ontario)	25th Battalion (Nova Scotia)	29th Battalion (British Columbia)
21st Battalion (Eastern Ontario)	26th Battalion (New Brunswick)	31st Battalion (Alberta)

3RD CANADIAN DIVISION

7th Infantry Brigade	8th Infantry Brigade	9th Infantry Brigade
Royal Canadian Regiment (Nova Scotia)	1st Canadian Mounted Rifles (Saskatchewan)	43rd Battalion (Cameron Highlanders of Winnipeg)
Princess Patricia's Canadian Light Infantry (Eastern Ontario)	2nd Canadian Mounted Rifles (British Columbia)	52nd Battalion (New Ontario)
42nd Battalion (Black Watch of Montreal)	4th Canadian Mounted Rifles (Central Ontario)	58th Battalion (Central Ontario)
49th Battalion (Alberta)	5th Canadian Mounted Rifles (Quebec)	116th Battalion (Ontario County)

4TH CANADIAN DIVISION

10th Infantry Brigade	11th Infantry Brigade	12th Infantry Brigade
44th Battalion (Manitoba)	54th Battalion (Central Ontario)	38th Battalion (Eastern Ontario)
46th Battalion (Saskatchewan)	75th Battalion (Mississauga Horse)	72nd Battalion (Seaforth Highlanders of Vancouver)
47th Battalion (Western Ontario)	87th Battalion (Grenadier Guards of Montreal)	78th Battalion (Winnipeg Grenadiers)
50th Battalion (Alberta)	102nd Battalion (Central Ontario)	85th (Nova Scotia Highlanders)

THE BATTLE OF AMIENS 1918

HISTORICAL OVERVIEW

1917 had ended in complete disaster for the Allies. The slaughter at Passchendaele and the dramatic failure of the Cambrai Offensive had left them morally and physically exhausted. Although the United States had entered the War in 1917, their troops had only started to arrive and, by early 1918, had yet to have a military impact. Russia had been defeated by Germany, and with their surrender the Germans now had major reserves to throw against the Western Front. All Generals and soldiers knew sometime in the spring the Germans would utilize their manpower advantage, and launch a major offensive, somewhere, against the Allied line. The Germans would not wait any longer because they knew the arrival of a large number of U.S. troops would tip the scales in favour of the Allies. So once the winter weather improved, both the British and French knew they were in for a major battle. The question was when and where would it come.

During the winter of 1917-18 the British worked feverishly to strengthen their defences. They anticipated 1918 would be another year of stalemate on the Western front. As in 1915, 1916 and 1917 the Generals felt defence would triumph over offence. Still an intense foreboding permeated throughout the Allied line, from the front-line trench to the General's Chateau.

The Canadian Corps had returned to its old stomping ground north of Arras after the Battle of Passchendaele in November 1917. There they had replenished their ranks and started preparing the defences that they hoped would blunt the impending German Offensive. During that winter the men of the Canadian Corps dug 400 km of trenches, strung 480 km of barbed-wire, and constructed 200 machine-gun emplacements. From the Douai plain, east of Vimy, to Loos in the north the Canadians were ready. In addition there were major organizational changes. Each Canadian Battalion was reinforced by 100 men, the 4 battalions/brigade establishment was maintained when the British went to a 3 battalions/brigade system, and the complement of Engineers and machine-gunners was increased in each Canadian Division. Consequently when one Canadian Division attacked, there would be 50% more soldiers involved than with one British Division.

The German Offensive

On March 21st, 1918 at 4:40 am, the Germans attacked in
dense fog along a 90 km front from Cambrai in the north to Moy,
south of St. Quentin, in the south. Troops, from 58 German Divisions, overwhelmed the British front lines and smashed all
defences before them. The attack, launched primarily against the
British 3rd and 5th Armies, was beyond a massive victory; it was a
rout. Village after village fell. All available British soldiers were
thrown in to slow the onslaught. After only two days of fighting
the Germans had advanced 16 km!

North of the main assault, on the Arras-Lens front, the Canadian Corps watched on with great concern, but there was little they
could do but wait. In these early days of the March Offensive most
Canadians saw little action. Only the men of the Canadian Cavalry Brigade and Canadian Motor Machine Guns had any role in
the fighting.

The Canadian Cavalry Brigade, consisting of the Royal Canadian Dragoons, Lord Strathcona's Horse, Fort Garry Horse and the
Royal Canadian Horse Artillery, fought, both mounted and dismounted, against the Germans on the Somme. On March 23rd
and 24th, in small groups, they tried to stem the advance, and
fought a fighting retreat.

The Canadian Motor Machine Guns consisted of the 1st and
2nd C.M.M.G. Brigades, which included such units as the Yukon,
Eaton and Borden Motor Machine Gun Batteries. Like the Cavalry these men, driving armoured cars or trucks carrying
machine-gun crews in the back, fought a running battle with the
Germans. They would dismount and fire on the attackers and
escape to fight at another village or crossroad. Many did not escape
and were steamrolled by the advancing Germans, and their burnt-
out vehicles and bodies lay scattered in many fields and small
villages across the Somme region. The valiant "Motors" performed
heroically, and inflicted many casualties on the advancing Germans. They had a far greater impact than their small numbers
would have indicated.

Throughout March 24th to March 28th, 1918, the offensive
continued unabated. The Enemy had advanced more than 60 km,
and were within 20 km of the major centre of Amiens, potentially
splitting the French and British Armies, and maybe winning the

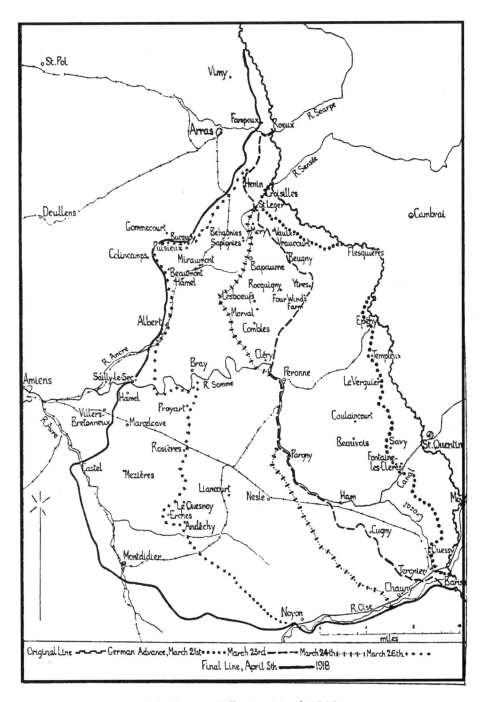

The German Offensive, March 1918

SPECIAL ORDER

By Lieutenant General Sir Arthur W. Currie, K.C.B.,K.C.M.G., Commanding Canadian Corps.
27th March, 1918

In an endeavour to reach an immediate decision the enemy has gathered all his forces and struck a mighty blow at the British Army. Overwhelmed by sheer weight of numbers the British Divisions in the line between the SCARPE and the OISE have fallen back fighting hard, steady and undismayed.

Measures have been taken successfully, to meet this German onslaught. The French have gathered a powerful Army, commanded by a most able and trusted leader and this Army is now moving swiftly to our help. Fresh British Divisions are being thrown in. The Canadians are soon to be engaged. Our Motor Machine Gun Brigade has already played a most gallant part and once again covered itself with glory.

Looking back with pride on the unbroken record of your glorious achievements, asking you to realize that today the fate of the British Empire hangs in the balance, I place my trust in the Canadian Corps, knowing that where Canadians are engaged there can be no giving way.

Under the orders of your devoted officers in the coming battle you will advance or fall where you stand facing the enemy.

To those who will fall I say, "You will not die but step into immortality. Your mothers will not lament your fate but will be proud to have borne such sons. Your names will be revered forever and ever by your grateful country and God will take you unto Himself."

Canadians, in this fateful hour, I command you and I trust you to fight as you have ever fought with all your strength, with all your determination, with all your tranquil courage. On many a hard fought field of battle you have overcome this enemy.

With God's help you shall achieve victory once more.

A. W. Currie
Lieutenant - General,
Commanding, Canadian Corps.

war. There were no signs that the Germans were slowing down. British casualties were heavy.

Back on the Canadian Corps front, General Currie issued his "Special Order", urging his men to fight on. On March 28th, 1918 the Germans finally launched an offensive against the Canadian positions north of Arras, but the defences in front of Vimy Ridge proved too much for them and the attack was quickly called off.

By March 30th the Germans had captured Villers-Bretonneux, 10 km east of Amiens. It seemed they were unstoppable. Their soldiers seemed to stream onwards, but no doubt the fatigue of a week's fighting, heavy losses, and stiffer Allied resolve had slowed their momentum. And it was near Villers-Bretonneux, that one of the bravest small actions of the war helped stem the German advance. The troops of the Canadian Cavalry Brigade launched a mounted charge on the Germans at Moreuil Wood. Led by Lieutenant Gordon Flowerdew of the Lord Strathcona's, the mounted Canadians charged the Germans in the Wood. Fighting was hand-to-hand but finally the Canadian Cavalry captured it. The losses were heavy and Moreuil Wood held only until the next day, but the courageous charge had brought some respite (See "Tour of Moreuil Wood").

By the end of March 1918, a combination of British, French and Australian reinforcements and German exhaustion had stalled the advance. On April 5th, 1918 the last German attack was made. It faltered and Amiens had been saved.

The British losses in March were more than 165,000 killed, wounded and prisoners. It was a horrific battle. By contrast Canadian casualties for March 1918 were only 2,749, of which 762 were soldiers from the Canadian Cavalry or Motor Machine-Guns.

In April and May the Germans launched major offensives elsewhere on the Western Front, and the Amiens front settled down. Whatever the territorial gains the Germans had made, they had lost the battle. It was an all or nothing venture and they had failed to crack the Allies. The net result, beyond the German losses, was a series of large and vulnerable salients in the Allied lines. The Germans did not have the men to defend the salients nor to properly fortify them. They were ripe for the picking.

At the end of the March Offensive Canadian Divisions were still holding some portion of the line from Arras to Lens. By April 1918 one Canadian Infantry Division was almost twice as strong as a British one (when you consider a shortage of British reinforcements and the Canadian organizational changes). The Germans were also aware the Canadians had not been heavily involved in the fighting. So the presence of the Canadian Corps in the line, indicated the probable location of any upcoming British attack. So it was at Arras that the Germans thought the Allies would start their counter-offensive.

At the end of June 1918, thousands of km from the Western Front, an event took place that would influence the Canadian's actions in the Battle of Amiens. On a return voyage to Liverpool from Halifax, the Hospital Ship (H.S.) Llandovery Castle was torpedoed by a German U-boat, 180 km south-west of the Fastnet. The ship sank but many of its crew, and most its medical staff escaped to lifeboats. However the German U-boat Commander decided there would be no survivors and machine-gunned the lifeboats. The Germans killed 234, including 88 Canadian Army Medical personnel. This was bad enough, but 14 of the dead were Canadian Nursing Sisters. Throughout the Empire there was a call for Revenge! (See "The Llandovery Castle".)

The Move South

On July 21st, 1918, General Currie was notified his men were to be part of a major attack against German positions opposite Amiens, with the objective to free the Amiens-Paris railway (also reffered to as the Villers-Bretonneux railway). It was critical the movement of the Canadian Corps from Arras be in complete secrecy. To divert the attention of the Germans, two Canadian Infantry Battalions and a Signals Company were sent to the Ypres front, near Kemmel. In the meantime the four Canadian Divisions, artillery, etc.; 100,000 men, were moved south to positions west of Amiens. There were some problems with the planned attack. The Canadians were not familiar with the lay of the land or the nature of the opposing defences, and by arriving during the first week in August, had only a few days to investigate them. But there were also many positives. Covering their northern flank would be the dependable Australians, and three Divisions of cavalry and 400 tanks were allotted for the offensive. In addition the German defences were vulnerable. They consisted primarily of unconnected trenches, many machine-gun positions, and very little barbed wire. The terrain was not destroyed by years of shelling, as had been the case in previous battles; mobility would not be a problem. Many of the German units in the line were under strength and exhausted after the spring offensive.

The Plan

The objective of the attack was to reduce the salient formed during the March Offensive, and free the Amiens-Paris railway. The attack would involve French and British Troops on the flanks, with the honour of the main assaults going to the Australian and Canadian Corps. The Offensive would be launched on a front of 18 km, from Ville-sur-Ancre in the north to Moreuil in the south. More than 400 tanks and three Cavalry Divisions were made available to exploit any breakthrough. A breakthrough was expected based on the French success at Soissons on July 18th, 1918.

The Canadian Corps Battle Front extended from the Amiens-Chaulnes (Villers-Bretonneux) railway in the north to a point 700 metres south of the village of Hourges in the south. It was a 8 km front. The Canadians were ordered to capture the old outer defences of Amiens, roughly 13 km east, from the jump-off line. It was an ambitious plan.

To reach their goal the Canadian Corps would employ all four Divisions on the first day of the attack. The first phase would involve overrunning the German's forward defences, 3 km deep. The second phase would continue the attack with the assistance of tanks to overcome any resistance or exploit any opportunities. Mounted cavalry, and motorized units would then follow through to the objective. To cover the Corps' northern flank all attacks would be synchronized with the Australians. The southern flank would be protected by the Canadian Independent Force; the C.M.M.G.Brigades, Canadian Light Horse, Cyclists and some truck-mounted trench mortars. They would race down the Amiens-Roye road and disrupt the Germans at every opportunity.

The operations were code-named "L.C." (Llandovery Castle), and thirst for vengeance and the frustration of waiting 7 months to fight brought the anticipation of battle to a feverish pitch. August 8th was to be their day and God help any Germans that got in their way.

The Canadian line ran from the Villers-Bretonneux railway in the north to a point 700 metres south of the Roye road in the

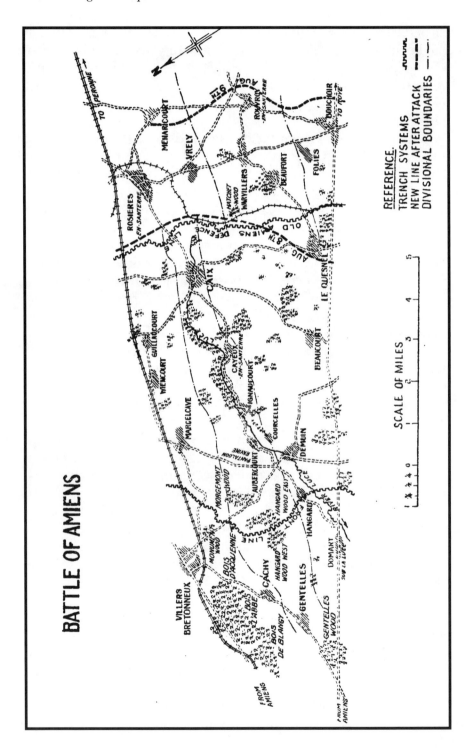

BATTLE OF AMIENS

REFERENCE.
TRENCH SYSTEMS
NEW LINE AFTER ATTACK
DIVISIONAL BOUNDARIES

SCALE OF MILES

south, a distance of 8 km. For the initial attack the Corps would use three Divisions; the 1st, 2nd and 3rd. The 2nd Canadian Division would attack along a 1,600 metre front, just south of the Australians; the 1st in the centre, on a 3,000 metre front and the 3rd Canadian Division was to attack on a 2,500 metre front south of the 1st Division. French troops and the Canadian Independent Force would operate south of the 3rd Division. The 4th Division would leap-frog the 3rd later in the attack.

The ground that opposed the Canadians consisted of a rolling plateau (Santerre) cut diagonally by the Luce River valley. The area surrounding the river is marshy and impassable to troops. Consequently the whole of the 3rd Division's attack would have to be funnelled over the Luce bridge east of Hourges. They had to negotiate the Luce River valley and fan out to continue the attack. In addition, the German Division opposing them was at strength and fully rested. The terrain over which the Canadians would advance consisted of bare slopes of farm land cut by numerous ravines with woods and copses scattered over the area. The Canadian part of the assault was critical.

The 2nd Division would attack parallel to the railway with the Australians protecting their northern flank. The 18th (Western Ontario) and the 19th (Central Ontario) Battalions would lead. The 21st (Eastern Ontario), the 26th (New Brunswick) and the 24th (Queen Victoria's Rifles of Montreal) would follow through to capture the strong points at Marcelcave and other small villages. For the final phase of the 2nd Division attack the 29th (British Columbia) and the 31st (Alberta) Battalions would carry the advance to its final objective near Harbonnieres.

It was critical during the attack that the 2nd Division keep up with the Australians or vice versa depending on the flow of battle. German machine-gunners would exploit any exposed flank, and would inflict devastating casualties on the assaulting troops.

The 1st Division would attack in the centre. It employed the 14th (Royal Montreal Regiment), the 13th (Black Watch of Montreal) and the 16th (Western Canadian Scottish) in the initial assault. The 13th Battalion had the unenviable task of capturing German fortifications in the Hangard Woods. In the second phase of the attack the 2nd (Eastern Ontario), 3rd (Toronto Regiment) and the 4th (Central Ontario) would carry the advance across and through the rolling farm lands and copses. The final phase of the advance would be carried by the 7th (British Columbia) and the 10th (Alberta) Battalions. If all went well these units would have advanced almost 13 km from the morning jump-off line, and captured Caix and the outer Amiens defence line.

The 3rd Division would have the most difficult attack to make. It would have to negotiate swampy regions around the Luce River between the villages of Hourges, Demuin and Hangard. To get to the jump-off points men of the 3rd Division had to be funnelled over the bridge at Domart. The leading battalions of the 3rd Division were the 1st Canadian Mounted Rifles (Saskatchewan) opposite Hangard, and the 58th (Central Ontario), 116th (Ontario County) and the 43rd (Cameron Highlanders of Winnipeg). Due to the confines placed by the Luce River Valley all three of the latter Battalions would launch their attack from a small area east of Hourges. They would then fan out to capture Hamon and Rifle Woods, and Mezieres. The 42nd (Black Watch of Montreal), 49th (Alberta) and the Royal Canadian Regiment would then leap-frog and continue the assault. British Cavalry was available to exploit any successes made by the Canadian attack.

The 4th Division would take over the attack from the 3rd west of Beaucourt village and attack German positions from Le Quesnel to Caix. They would employ the 54th (Central Ontario), and the 102nd (Central Ontario) to capture Beaucourt and Beaucourt Wood and the 75th (Mississauga Horse) and the 87th (Grenadier Guards of Montreal) to take Le Quesnel. In the north the 72nd (Seaforth Highlanders of Vancouver), 78th (Winnipeg Grenadiers) and the 85th (Nova Scotia Highlanders) to take the objectives south of Caix.

The Battle Opens

At 4:20 am on August 8th, 1918, the noise of a thousand guns firing split the quiet, and an immense barrage enveloped the German positions in a sheet of flame. Into a thick mist Canadian, Australian, British and French troops climbed out of their trenches and moved on. The sound of 400 tanks, the clinking of their caterpillar tracks, and roaring of their diesel engines added a monsterous din to the hellish spectacle. The Battle of Amiens was on.

The 2nd Division's attack across the Santerre plateau went well. Advancing quickly, with the aid of a misty morning, they over ran the German trenches, capturing many machine-guns and prisoners. The 21st Battalion captured Marcelcave and the supporting battalions passed through to carry the attack. With little resistance the men of the 2nd Division captured the villages of Wiencourt and Guillaucourt and reached the objective east of Caix. By early evening the 2nd Division was in the Amiens defence line, right on schedule. They had advanced almost 13 km!

The early morning mist also assisted the attack of the 1st Division. The 13th Battalion assaulted Hangard Wood and in a stiff fight overwhelmed the Germans. Acts of individual courage greatly assisted in the success of the attack. Private John Croak attacked and single-handedly captured a German machine-gun post, and although seriously wounded, attacked and captured 3 more. Croak was wounded again in the second assault and died of his wounds. Corporal H. Good, also of the 13th Battalion captured 3 German machine guns and then a German artillery battery and crew. Both Croak and Good were awarded the Victoria Cross.

Canadian armoured cars going into action. Battle of Amiens. August 9th, 1918

(PUBLIC ARCHIVES OF CANADA PA-3016)

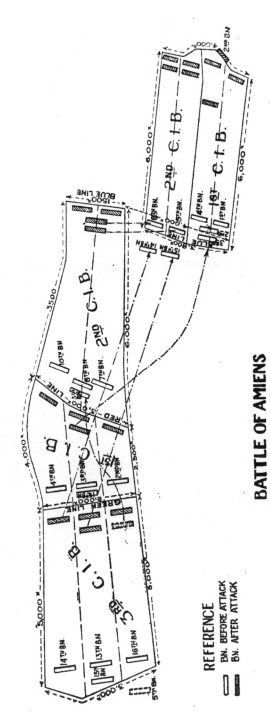

BATTLE OF AMIENS

DIAGRAM SHOWING EMPLOYMENT OF INFANTRY

Employment of 1st Canadian Division August 8th, 1918.

The 1st Division's attack was so successful and so quick even German artillery was captured in place. Their advance by-passed many pockets of the enemy who later created many problems for the supporting battalions. Once out of the woods the 3rd and 4th Battalions moved rapidly across the rolling farmland, being lightly opposed. Only the fire of isolated German machine-guns occassionally, and briefly, held up the advance.

All enemy resistance had been quashed and by the early afternoon the 10th Battalion captured Caix. The 1st Division had successfully completed its assignment.

The leading battalions on the 3rd Division's front, greatly assisted by tanks, had completely surprised the Germans. The 43rd and 116th Battalions had quickly taken their objectives, capturing many prisoners. The 1st CMR, attacking opposite Hangard had succeeded in taking the village and pushing across the Luce River south of Demuin. It was an astonishing advance. A little after 8 am the Royal Canadian Regiment, 49th and 42nd Battalions continued the assault. They drove on, both along the Amiens-Roye road and across the fields east of Demuin. Before noon the 3rd Division had succeeded in capturing all its assignments.

The Canadian Independent Force had also had a successful morning, using its great mobility to advance along the Amiens-Roye road. British cavalry and tanks added to the general euphoria. There had never been a victory like this.

The Royal Canadian Dragoons attacked over the open fields, the same fields they had retreated over in March. They captured Beaucourt, and the Canadian troops cheered as they watched the cavalry move eastwards, on towards more quarry. As the 4th Division picked-up the attack on Le Quesnel there was a perceptible change in the resistance of the Germans. The chattering of enemy machine-guns was more pronounced and the proud cavalry were reminded that horses are no match for bullets. None-the-less the men of the 54th and 102nd Battalions rushed and captured Beaucourt Wood, but were held up in the open fields west of Le Quesnel. On their left or northern flank the 78th, 72nd and 85th Battalions captured their objectives on the outer Amiens defence line. It was getting late in the day and heavy machine-gun fire from south of the Amiens-Roye road was still pinning down the attackers of the 75th Battalion in the fields. As darkness fell upon the battlefield, it was clear the capture of Le Quesnel would have to wait.

Finally the advance of August 8th, 1918 was over. It had been an unparalleled success. Only at Le Quesnel had the Canadians failed to take their objective, and certainly it would fall the next day. The Australians had also had a successful day, however the British had been stopped cold by the Germans on the northern flank of the offensive.

August 8th had cost the Canadian Corps 3,868 casualties, including 1,036 dead. They had captured more than 5,000 prisoners. The Llandovery Castle had been avenged.

Day Two; August 9th, 1918.
On August 9th the opportunity for another victory was still there for the Canadians. There could be no element of surprise, the attackers would have fewer tanks and less artillery support. There were also more German reinforcements arriving by the minute. But the momentum still favoured the attackers. August 9th, 1918 would be Canadian infantry and tanks against German machine-guns. The first priority for the Canadians was to capture Le Quesnel, and at 4:30 am the 75th and 87th Battalions attacked the village and the woods around it. The Germans put up a spirited defence, but the infantry, with the assistance of Canadian armoured cars took the stronghold by noon.

The delay in taking Le Quesnel and the general confusion following August 8th's great advance caused the plans for Day Two to be changed. Finally when the orders were given the day was half gone, and the Divisional assignments were revised accordingly. The revised plan was to attack on a 8 km front with the three Divisions in the line; 2nd (northern flank), 1st (centre), and 3rd (southern flank). The Divisions were to advance 5 km to the line, Mehari-court-Rouvroy-Bouchoir. The terrain was flat, with a few villages and woods. German defences were considered light, but no one knew exactly where they were. This was a war of mobility, and victory was dependent on courage and initiative.

Due to the confusion caused by the revised schedules each Division jumped-off at different times. The 2nd Division attacked with the 29th and 31st Battalions at 11:00 am, and quickly captured Rosieres. The 27th (City of Winnipeg) and 28th (Saskatchewan) Battalions continued the attack, and with the assistance of tanks and the Australians, took all their objectives. South of that attack,

German dead killed during the Canadian advance. Battle of Amiens. August, 1918

the 22nd (French-Canadian) and the 25th (Nova Scotia) Battalions, also of the 2nd Division, fought across the open fields and into the village of Vrely. They pushed on against the Germans in Meharicourt, and it was during this action that the Van-doos won their second Victoria Cross of the war. Lieutenant Jean Brillant was mortally wounded near Meharicourt, but his bravery contributed to the success of the operation. By 5:00 pm the 2nd Division had succeeded along the line.

The 1st Division attacked just south of the 2nd Division, and did so without tank or artillery support. They jumped-off at 1:10 pm. In the face of heavy machine-gun fire the men of the 5th (Saskatchewan) and 8th (90th Rifles of Winnipeg) Battalions, using the courage and ingenuity of its men, outmanoeuvred the German outposts in Hatchet Wood, pushed across the open fields, and captured Warvillers village. Three Victoria Crosses were awarded for the action; R. L. Zengel (of the 5th Battalion), F.C Coppins and A. Brereton (both of the 8th Battalion).

The southern attack of the 1st Division was led by the 2nd (Eastern Ontario) and 1st (Western Ontario) Battalions who battled

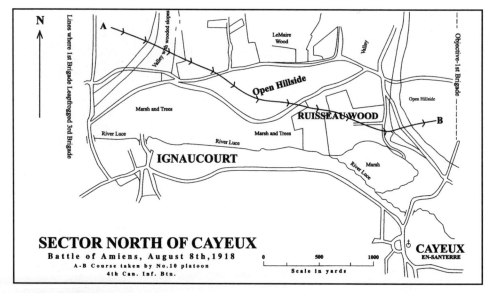

Area of attack - 4th Canadian Infantry Battalion, August 8th, 1918.

the Germans north of Le Quesnel, and captured Beaufort village. The 2nd and 4th (Central Ontario) Battalions then joined hands and took Rouvroy. Fighting in the village was severe and it was not until 9:00 pm that the village was cleared.

The attack of the 3rd Division had to wait until Le Quesnel was cleared, so was not launched until 2:00 pm. It was a simple plan that employed two battalions; the 4th (Central Ontario) Canadian Mounted Rifles, and the 5th (Quebec) CMR attacking along the Amiens-Roye road. They captured (with the assistance of tanks) the villages of Folies and Bouchoir. In three hours they had completed all their assignments.

Day Two was a great achievement, although not like August 8th. The Canadian Corps had advanced more than 6 km. But the second day had also been costly; another 2,574 Canadian soldiers were wounded or dead.

Day Three; August 10th, 1918.

The impetus of the battle had waned by Day Three. The Germans had brought in six fresh Divisions to face the Canadians, and a new attitude; hold at all costs. This meant any advance would be met by stiff and numerous counter-attacks, in the German tradition. Secondly, and at least as important, the attackers were faced with the old 1916 Somme defences. They had served as the front lines in 1916, and had been abandoned in 1917. They were parallel to the Canadian lines and 5 km deep, incorporating into them; old trenches, tunnels, barbed-wire, pitted shell-holes, and several villages. They offered a formidable defence for the German machine-gunners.

The 4th Division were given the unpleasant job of breaking into the old Somme defences. They would employ the 72nd (Seaforth Highlanders of Vancouver), 38th (Eastern Ontario) and the 85th (Nova Scotia Highlanders) Battalions to capture the area from the Villers-Bretonneux railway to Maucourt village. The 46th (Saskatchewan) and 47th (Western Ontario) would attack between Maucourt and Fouquescourt. The dubious privilege of taking Fouquescourt was given to the 44th (Manitoba) Battalion.

At 4:15 am the 4th Division launched its assault across the open fields swept by machine-gun fire, in front of the old trenches. They attacked with much courage, but also anxiety, as no one knew anything about the positions they were attacking. Very little progress was made against the old trenches, until the 72nd Battalion captured Maucourt and Chilly, allowing the German trenches to be entered from the northern flank. Finally the 44th Battalion fought its way through Fouquescourt, and the 47th Battalion joined them. Together they pushed east of the village and extended the line north. The success of the 72nd Battalion was followed on by the 78th (Winnipeg Grenadiers) Battalion, who captured Hallu. Lieutenant James Tait led his men forwards against heavy odds, and for his bravery was awarded the Victoria Cross. By the evening of August 10th, 1918 the Canadians were firmly entrenched in the old Somme defences, but fierce counter-attacks continued, and only the determined efforts of small groups of Canadian soldiers held back the Germans.

The fighting of August 10th, 1918 marked the last major assault by the Canadian Corps in the Battle of Amiens. But the fighting was not finished. Over the next week the 3rd Canadian Division fought many small actions in an attempt to clear the old 1916 trench system. The fighting was always confused and bitter, pitting one small group of Canadians against another small group of Germans. Between August 12th-14th there were several sharp actions in the old trenches near Fouquescourt and Parvillers. Patrols of the Princess Patricia's Canadian Light Infantry, 42nd

Tanks advancing. Prisoners bring in wounded wearing gas masks. Battle of Amiens. Amiens, France. August 1918.

(Black Watch of Montreal) and 52nd (New Ontario) Battalions fought running battles with the Germans; winning some ground only to lose it in a vicious counter-attack. It was during actions such as this that two Canadians (R. Spall of the PPCLI and T. Dinesen of the 42nd Battalion) won the Victoria Cross. Through pure tenacity the villages of Damery and Parvillers fell to the Canadians on August 15th, 1918.

Battalions of the 1st and 2nd Divisions relieved the 3rd Division on August 16th and were immediately drawn into local actions in the villages of Fresnoy-les-Roye and La Chavatte. Both villages were firmly in Canadian hands on the 17th. Later that week the first Canadians were withdrawn from the lines and moved to the Arras front.

On August 22nd, 1918 Sir Arthur Currie, the General commanding the Canadian Corps, officially handed over the Canadian Corps front, and closed his Headquarters.

The Battle of Amiens was a major turning point in the First World War, and it was a honour the Canadian Corps were asked to play such a decisive role. The Battle had cost the Canadians 11,822

Canadians digging in and waiting for the next wave to pass through them and go forward. Battle of Amiens. August 1918.

(PUBLIC ARCHIVES OF CANADA PA-2926)

killed and wounded. They had captured 9,131 Germans, and penetrated 23 km into German-held territory. The Canadian Corps had once again proved its efficiency by spearheading the greatest British victory of the war to date. They had arrived on the Amiens front without the slightest understanding of the terrain, the enemy's position, nor the enemy himself, and had achieved incredible results. The battered Corps was on the move again and within a week would launch another major offensive against the formidable Hindenburg line east of Arras. It would be their greatest victory of the war.

TOUR ITINERARY
Duration 7.5 hours

Point 1: *Crucifix Corner Cemetery; the attack of the 2nd Division, August 8th, 1918*

Point 2: *Hangard Woods, East and West; the attack of the 1st Division, August 8th, 1918*

Point 3: *Hourges Orchard Cemetery; the attack of the 3rd Division, August 8th, 1918*

Point 4: *Hill 102; the advance of the 3rd Division continues, August 8th, 1918*

Point 5: *Le Quesnel Canadian Battlefield Memorial; the attack of the 4th Division, August 8th, 1918*

Point 6: *Manitoba Cemetery; the attack of the 1st Division, August 9th, 1918*

Point 7: *Fouquescourt British Cemetery; the attack of the 4th Division, August 10th, 1918*

Point 8: *Parvillers; the assault of the 3rd Division, August 12th-15th, 1918*

Point 9: *Toronto Cemetery; the advance of the 1st Division continues, August 8th, 1918*

THE BATTLE OF AMIENS 1918

THE TOUR

The Battle of Amiens was a tremendously successful battle by First World War standards. Unlike the Battles of Ypres, the Somme or Passchendaele, where the whole battlefield is a walk, the Battle of Amiens covers ten times more territory and is a driving tour. There are many points of interest and I have selected only a few to cover the entire battlefield.

The tour starts in the Grande Place in Arras. Follow the road signs leading to Cambrai (D939) and the main toll (peage) highway to Paris and Lille, the A1-E15. Take the D939 exiting Arras in the south-east, passing the village of Tilloy-les-Mofflaines (the scene of heavy fighting in 1917 and a jump-off point for the Canadian Corps in 1918); after 7 km you reach a round-about, take the left exit and get on the A1-E15 heading south to Paris. Continue on the Autoroute for 43 km, passing the exit for Bapaume, (exit 14). Take the next exit (Peronne and St.Quentin, exit 15), and follow the N29-E44 west to Amiens. Once off the Autoroute you are 39 km from Amiens and driving along a plateau, and through the area captured by the Australians on August 8th to 10th, 1918. It is an excellent view of the Amiens battlefield. The Canadians battlefields are 7 km south (your left) of the N29-E44. Continue on the road for 23 km until the village of Villers-Bretonneux is reached. The D23 crosses the N29-E44 (in the middle of the village). Turn left on the D23 to Demuin to start the Canadian Battlefield tour. (However, it is worthwhile to start your tour by visiting the Australian National Memorial 2 km north of the village on the D23. It is the equivalent of the Canadian National Memorial at Vimy and an incredible view of the battlefields can be obtained from the top of the Memorial Tower.)

After 2 km driving south on the D23 Crucifix Corner Cemetery appears on your right. Stop at the cemetery.

Demuin Village from Demuin British Cemetery

Point 1: Crucifix Corner Cemetery, the attack of the 2nd Division.

The role of the 2nd Canadian Division was to keep up with the advance of the Australians, who were on their immediate left. The

2nd Division employed 2 battalions, the 18th and 19th for the initial assault. The terrain that opposed them was a plateau, still covered with farmer's crops, with small woods providing deadly obstacles for the attackers.

Walk to the back of the cemetery.

Looking 1000 metres west and north you can see where the Canadian front lines were. At 4:20 am the men of the 18th (Western Ontario) and 19th (Central Ontario) battalions attacked across the open field in front of you. The 18th advanced rapidly through the location where you are now standing, and pushed through limited resistance for another 4 km to the village of Marcelcave (due east). The 19th Battalion on the right, jumped-off from a bend in the German lines roughly 400 metres north of where you stand. The advance was held up by heavy machine-gun fire from a number of German trenches near the railway embankment (the Canadian sector for the whole attack was from the railway line, Amiens-Chaulnes, in the north to just south of the Amiens-Roye road (D934) in the south. The Australian Corps operated north of the railway and the French attacked south of the D934). The resistance could not deter the attackers and by 6:30 am the 19th, and 18th Battalions, now assisted by the 21st Battalion had captured Marcelcave. The first phase of the attack was a complete success.

Return to your car and continue towards Demuin on the D23. You are crossing the lines of advancing Canadian troops. Men of the 14th (Royal Montreal Regiment) and the 13th (Black Watch of Montreal) fought across this road, captured the wood on your left (Morgemont Wood) after overcoming stiff resistance from German machine-gun nests. To your right, opposite Morgemont wood you can see Hangard Wood (East), the scene of fierce fighting when the battle opened (see Point 3). Continue on the D23 as it dips into the Luce River valley. After 3.5 km a small Canadian cemetery (Demuin British Cemetery) appears on your right, roughly 100 metres past the cemetery turn right on the D76 to Hangard. You are now driving through the area captured by the 1st Canadian Mounted Rifles (Saskatchewan) in the early morning of August 8th, 1918. After 1.25 km Hangard Communal Cemetery Extension is passed, continue on into the village. In the centre of the village watch for the sign posts to Hangard Wood British Cemetery. Turn right on the small road

The view of Hangard Woods from Point 2. Hangard Wood Cemetery is in the foreground, between the woods (PHOTO: N. CHRISTIE)

leading north of the village. The road will climb up a ridge and at the crest of the ridge stop your car. The view to the north is of two woods, Hangard Wood West (left) and East(right). They mark the front lines of the Canadians and Germans, and were the scene of the heaviest fighting on August 8th. They are also the place where two Canadian Victoria Crosses were won.

Point 2: Hangard Woods, East and West; the attack of the 1st Canadian Division.

The German lines ran along the western face of Hangard Wood East with advance posts halfway into Hangard Wood West. The Canadian lines ran through the western half of the wood. The 1st Division was given the task of capturing the Woods. They employed the 13th Battalion in the Wood and the 16th (Canadian Scottish) Battalion against the Germans between the Wood and where you now stand. The attack of the 16th went well and they did not encounter much resistance until they hit the D23 (where you turned towards Hangard). However they quickly pushed the enemy back, and advanced, pushing 1000 metres east of Demuin village,

Demuin Corps H.Q. during Amiens offensive. 1919.
(Hangard Woods are in the background)

(PUBLIC ARCHIVES OF CANADA PA-4542)

where they captured a German Regimental Commander and his staff. Many of their dead lie in Demuin British Cemetery.

The advance was not so easy for the 13th Battalion. The advance German positions in Hangard Wood West inflicted heavy casualties on the 13th and were endangering the success of the Canadian attack. In the end it was the bravery of individual soldiers, using initiative and courage that overcame the Germans. Private John Croak[1], single-handed, attacked and silenced a machine-gun position, and although severely wounded attacked another German strong point and bayonetted the crew. Croak was mortally wounded in the second assault and died of his wounds. He is buried in Hangard Wood Cemetery, Plot I, Row A, Grave 9.

Similar courage was displayed by Corporal Herman Good[2], who charged three German machine-guns and killed or captured the crews.

---

[1] John Bernard Croak; born Little Bay, Newfoundland, May 18, 1892; died Hangard Wood, August 8, 1918.

[2] Herman James Good; born South Bathurst, New Brunswick, November 29, 1887; died Bathurst, New Brunswick, April 18, 1969.

The 16th Battalion at Demuin.

The following was extracted from "The History of the 16th Battalion (The Canadian Scottish)" by H.M. Urqhuart. It describes the attack made by the 16th Battalion at the start of the battle, when it advanced north of Demuin village. Many of those killed in this action are buried in Demuin British Cemetery.

"Seven tanks in two sections were allotted to the Battalion, and one mobile brigade of Field Artillery accompanied the 1st Division's attack to take on targets after the main barrage had ceased.

"The wide No Man's Land, which the unit had first to traverse, was untouched by the shell fire. It was soon crossed. Paths had been cut through the enemy's wire and it afforded no obstacle; but on approaching nearer to the German defences progress became less rapid. The supporting artillery barrage had struck here in its full force, the smell of the newly torn earth rose strong from the ground; the fumes of the high explosives and the smoke screen, held close down by the clammy fog, got into the men's eyes and throats and caused them to stumble, lose sense of direction and group together. The consequent confusion was in no wise improved by the arrival of the tanks which lunged around in a disconcerning way.

"The story of the fighting in the enemy's outpost zone is therefore disconnected. It relies upon the narratives of leaders not co-operating with each other, although, in themselves, these give a fairly accurate idea of the general characteristics of the attack at that stage of the battle.

"We passed through to the south of 'Strip Copse'," proceeds one account, *"and down the hill in front of us at a location which I judge to be between Vear Alley and Wren Copse I could see something that looked like an emplacement. Piper Maclean of Number 2 Company was with my party at the time. I told him to play 'The Drunken Piper', and to the strains of this tune, played in quick time, we charged. It was an emplacement sure enough, of heavy trench mortars. Jumping into the trench we saw in front of us the entrances to two dug-outs each guarded with a machine gun mounted and well camouflaged. We shouted down to the enemy and up they came--one officer and about sixty men. They were taken completely by surprise; some of them were in their stocking feet and partly clad. Arrived above ground they seemed determined to 'dish up' their day's rations, and make themselves comfortable before starting the journey to the rear, but after some gentle (?) Persuasion we settled that matter and sent them quickly on their way at the double. Soon after, to the north-*

east of Cemetery Copse we ran into another party of Germans, about twenty in number, and hurried them back."

"All went well with us at the start," runs another description of the fighting more to the left of the Battalion's front. *"We had advanced seven to eight hundred yards without meeting any of the enemy and were passing through a field of rye, when suddenly somebody rose up right in*

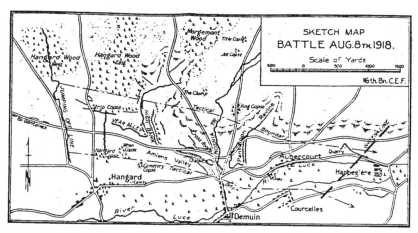

front of me. I stopped, told the men to get down, and challenged. The man in front ran so I fired dropping him. I doubled ahead, followed by the platoon and found a big German shot through the face, breathing his last. On looking round I discovered two more of the enemy standing watching us from a 'T' head listening post. They surrendered without a fight, were sent back, and again we advanced, but had not gone far when I heard a noise in front and running ahead caught sight of a Hun setting up a machine gun. I shot him, and the section corporal and myself jumped into a short trench, which we found led to a trench mortar battery--a most elaborate emplacement--in a clump of trees close by. Looking around we discovered the entrance to a deep dug-out down which I shouted and up came an officer and about thirty men. I called for a volunteer to take the prisoners back but no one wished to go. I was on the point of detailing a man for the duty when conveniently two of Number 4 Company, with a big lot of Germans, passed us and I attached our group to them."

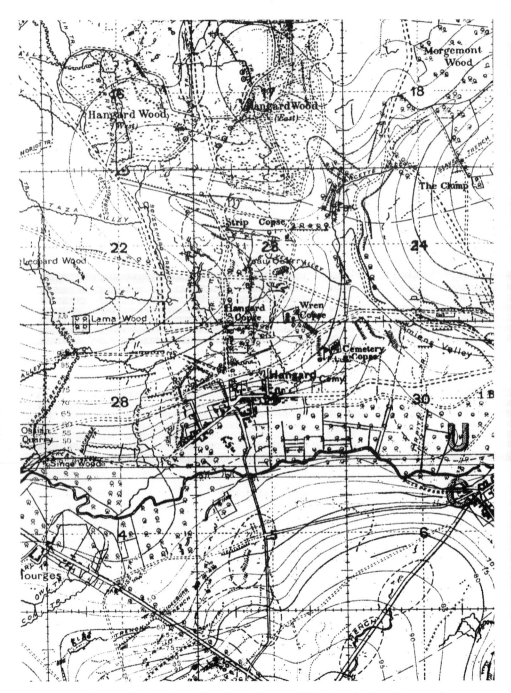

Trench map showing front lines from Hangard Woods to Amiens-Roye road.

Later in the battle, Good and 3 others, rushed a German artillery battery. The attack of only four Canadians on a considerably larger number of unprepared German artillerymen was sufficient to produce an immediate surrender. There was no doubt the Canadians' blood was up.

Both John Croak and Herman Good were awarded the Victoria Cross for their courageous actions.

With great ferocity the 13th Battalion captured Hangard Wood West and encircled the Germans in the East Wood. There was no time to rest and the 13th pushed on across the D23 and past Morgemont Wood.

Return to Hangard and turn right on the D76 to Domart-sur-la-Luce. It is important to note that the success of the Canadian attack was held in the Luce River Valley (the Luce is on your left). The Germans had fresh troops in the line and easy territory to defend. Continue 1.6 km to Domart. The area you are driving through was ensconced in mist at 4:20 am on August 8th, 1918. To your left is the ground the 58th (Central Ontario) Battalion captured in the early morning and on your right was the territory captured by the 1st CMR. When the D76 meets the D934 turn left to Hourges. After 80 metres you will drive over the bridge on the Luce River. It was at this location that thousands of Canadian soldiers crossed the river to move up for the assault. It was heavily shelled on August 8th. On your right is Hourges Orchard Cemetery. Drive to the cemetery and stop.

Point 3: Hourges Orchard Cemetery; the attack of the 3rd Division.

You are standing in what was the jump-off trench of the 116th (Ontario County) Battalion on August 8th, 1918. The German lines, a scattering of disconnected trenches were 500 metres east of where you stand.

The attack of the 3rd Canadian Division was more complex than the attack of the other two Divisions. It included a crucial, and difficult assault, of sweeping up the Luce River Valley. The task of capturing the Luce River Valley was given to the 58th (Central Ontario) Battalion. It would require them to overcome the Germans in the small ravines coming off the valley. They jumped-off just north of the D934, north of the hamlet of Hourges, 500 metres north west of where you stand. Their attack was along the Hangard road, through the area you just drove across.

When the 58th delivered the attack at 4:20 am the valley was
shrouded in mist which greatly helped in surprising the Germans,
but did not help keeping the correct direction of the Canadian
attack. Greatly assisted by tanks the 58th quickly captured the valley and the village of Demuin. Corporal Harry Miner[3] of the 58th
Battalion, although wounded, single-handedly, captured a
machine-gun, killed its crew and turned the gun on the retreating
Germans. Later in the day he rushed and captured two other German strong points. In the assault, near Demuin, Miner was again
wounded, this time mortally. He was removed to a Casualty Clearing Station, but died of his wounds later that day. For his bravery
Harry Miner was posthumously awarded the Victoria Cross. He
rests in Crouy British Cemetery, Plot V, Row B, Grave 11.

The other battalions of the 3rd Division's 9th Brigade were
equally successful. The 116th, who along with the other attacking
battalions, had only moved into the line at 2 am that morning had
met stiff resistance from Dodo Wood (1 km down the D934, on
your right), but continued the advance down the D934. They captured Hamon Wood, 2 km down the D934, it is the large wood on
your left. By 6:15 am they were 2.5 km from their jump-off lines.
The attack was then continued by the Royal Canadian Regiment
(RCR).

The 43rd (Cameron Highlanders of Winnipeg) Battalion
attacked south of the 116th. It successfully covered the right flank
of the Canadian attack. For the Battle of Amiens the Commander
of the Canadian Corps, Sir Arthur Currie, formed a highly mobile
unit, known as the Canadian Independent Force. The unit was
made up of the Motorized Machine gun batteries, the Canadian
Light Horse, Canadian Cyclists and two trench mortars.

This assortment of vehicles joined into the attack at 9:00 am
They drove their fragile armoured cars and trucks down D934 by
the cemetery where you stand and went in search of the enemy.
Throughout the day they assisted the infantry and played a major
role in the capture of Mezieres village, 5 km away. It was one of
the first uses of a motorized force in the history of war.

---

[3] Harry Garnet Bedford Miner; born Cedar Springs, Ontario, June 24, 1891; died Crouy,
France, August 8, 1918.

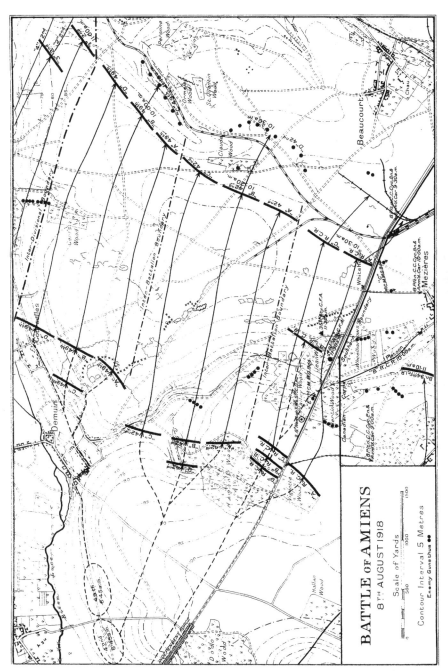

Attack of the 3rd Division; Second Phase, August 8th, 1918.

Return to your car and continue east on the D934 towards Roye. Continue on the road past Dodo Wood (on your right after 1km), past the intersection of the D23, to Demuin and Moreuil[4], past Hamon Wood, 1 km further on your left. After 5 km turn left on the D137 to Demuin and Ignaucourt. This crossroads was the scene of heavy fighting (then known as the Brickfields and White House). After 1.25 km the D137 swerves to the left, and meets 3 other small roads. Stop the car.

Point 4: Hill 102; the advance of the 3rd Division continues.

You are standing on what was known as Hill 102. It was captured before noon on August 8th, 1918 by the 42nd (Black Watch of Canada) Battalion. Looking west you can imagine the Canadians advancing across the open fields; the kilted Highlanders moving forward with the men of the 49th (Edmonton Regiment) Battalion on their flank. The church steeple in the village of Demuin can be seen to the north-west, just sticking out of the hollow made by the Luce River Valley. The village had been captured by the 58th Battalion earlier in the morning and the 42nd and 49th Battalions were continuing the attack. With the capture of Hill 102 two major objectives had been taken and only the third remained. So far it was an incredible day. The capture of the third objective had been allotted to the 4th Canadian Division. Eight battalions of the 4th Division, 5,000 Canadians, were moving forward across these fields towards the village of Beaucourt. To add colour, the 3rd British Cavalry Division, which contained the Canadian Cavalry Brigade (Fort Garry Horse, Lord Strathcona's Horse, Royal Canadian Dragoons and the Royal Canadian Horse Artillery), was also arriving to exploit the success of the 3rd Division's attack. They chased the retreating Germans through Beaucourt (the village to the east), but as they moved forward the German defences at Le Quesnel stiffened, and machine-guns stopped the cavalry advance. It appeared the 4th Division would have a much harder time than the 3rd.

Turn right on the small (unnumbered) road at the road junction, heading south-east to Beaucourt village. Continue through the village until the road ends. Turn left and then right on a small road, signposted to Beaucourt British Cemetery and Le Quesnel. Continue 3 km to Le Quesnel village and after 0.5 km

---

[4] To visit Moreuil Wood turn right on the D23 to Moreuil, after 2 km the Wood appears on your right. See the tour of Moreuil Wood on page 82.

Beaucourt from Le Quesnel Memorial   (PHOTO: N. CHRISTIE)

turn right on a small road leading south-west out of Le Quesnel. After 800 metres the Canadian Battlefield Memorial appears on your left. Stop at the Memorial.

Point 5: Le Quesnel Canadian Battlefield Memorial; the attack of the 4th Division.

The attack thus far had gone perfectly. By First World War standards the territory gained by the Canadians, and the Australians to the north, represented the greatest Allied victory in the war to date. Now it was up to the 4th Division, moving up to the attack, to finish the job and capture the final objective, Le Quesnel.

Launching their assault from the eastern edge of Beaucourt village (north-west of you), the 75th (Mississauga Horse) and the 54th (Central Ontario) Battalions attacked across the open fields between the D934 and Beaucourt village. The 102nd (Central Ontario) Battalion attacked Beaucourt Wood (the wood 750 metres north of where you now stand). By 4:35 pm the Wood was cleared but the 102nd suffered 111 dead or wounded. The attack by the 75th and 54th Battalions had met with severe resistance from machine-guns near Le Quesnel and could not advance. As night fell, they dug in across the fields 1 km north-west of you. The advance for August 8th, 1918 had ended and only at Le Quesnel did the Canadians fail to reach their objective. It does seem odd

THE LE QUESNEL CANADIAN MEMORIAL

The Canadian monument at Le Quesnel, 28 km east of the City of Amiens on the D934, stands on one of eight First World War Canadian battlefields officially commemorated.

In 1920, the Canadian Battlefield Monument Commission decided to erect memorials at:

St. Julien - to commemorate the Second Battle of Ypres
Hill 62 - to commemorate the Battle of Mount Sorrel
Courcelette - to commemorate the Battle of the Somme
Vimy - to commemorate the Battle of Vimy Ridge
Passchendaele - to commemorate the Battle of Passchendaele
Le Quesnel - to commemorate the Battle of Amiens
Dury - to commemorate the Battle of Arras 1918 and the capture of the Drocourt-Queant line
Bourlon Wood - to commemorate the Battles of the Canal du Nord, Cambrai, the capture of Valenciennes and Mons and the March to the Rhine

It was decided that Vimy would act as the National Memorial and have a unique design. The other seven would be marked with identical memorials. A competition was held to choose an architect to design the monuments. Walter Allward of Toronto was chosen for Vimy's unique memorial and Frederick C. Clemesha of Regina took second place. Clemesha's design, "The Brooding Soldier," was built at St. Julien and had such a stark effect at its unveiling in 1923 that the Monument Commission decided it also should remain unique.

In conjunction with the architectural advisor, P. E. Nobbs, the cube design was developed for the remaining six monuments. A 13-tonne block of Stanstead granite was used for each. A wreath was carved into two sides of the monument and on the other two sides was engraved a brief explanation of the exploits of the Canadian Corps in that specific battle. One side is in English, the other in French.

At Le Quesnel, the monument reads:

THE CANADIAN CORPS ONE HUNDRED THOUSAND STRONG ON 8TH AUGUST 1918 ATTACKED BETWEEN HOURGES AND VILLERS BRETONNEUX AND DROVE THE ENEMY EASTWARD FOR EIGHT MILES.

Around the base of the stone, it reads:

HONOUR TO CANADIANS WHO ON THE FIELDS OF FLANDERS AND OF FRANCE FOUGHT IN THE CAUSE OF THE ALLIES WITH SACRIFICE AND DEVOTION

Strangely the Memorial is located at the only objective NOT reached on August 8th, 1918! The Park is larger than most of the other Battlefield sites and has recently been renovated, so there are excellent views of Beaucourt Wood, Beaucourt, and Le Quesnel Wood. True to each of the Canadian Memorials, its inscription is anything but inspiring. Amiens was a major breaking point in the Great War, and the Canadians played the biggest part in its stunning success. Don't be deceived by the wording.

that the Canadian Government chose to put a National Battle-field Memorial at the only objective not taken on August 8th. North of Beaucourt Wood other battalions of the 4th Division successfully attacked and captured the area north of Le Quesnel. The 72nd (Seaforth Highlanders of Vancouver) and the 78th (Winnipeg Grenadiers) overcame all resistance and captured the ridge overlooking the village.

Return to Le Quesnel village and turn left on the D41 to Caix. As you drive along the D41 you are passing through territory captured by the 78th and 72nd Battalions. After 2 km Hillside Cemetery, one of the prettiest cemeteries in France, appears on your left. It is well worth a visit. Continue 2.5 km toward Caix (it was captured by the 10th (Alberta) Battalion). Just 500 metres south of the village turn right (almost back on yourself) on a small unnumbered road to Beaufort-en-Santerre, and signposted Manitoba Cemetery. The cemetery will appear on your left after 2 km. Stop your car and enter the cemetery.

Point 6: Manitoba Cemetery; the attack of the 1st Division, August 9th, 1918.

The Canadian plan for August 9th, 1918 was to keep pushing. Unfortunately for the attackers there could be no element of surprise and the Germans had reacted quickly by bringing seven divisions to reinforce the line. The plan for August 9th, was to continue the assault using the same divisions that had fought so hard the previous day. The Canadians jump-off line was 500 metres west of where you stand. At 10:00 am on August 9th, four battalions of the 1st Division attacked across the fields north and south of where you stand. The 5th (Saskatchewan) Battalion pushed south of you, driving on the village of Warvillers (2 km south-east), and the 8th (Winnipeg Rifles) advanced through the cemetery and the wood just east of you (Hatchet Wood). South of the 5th Battalion's attack the 2nd (Eastern Ontario) and the 4th (Central Ontario) Battalions moved against the German positions near the village of Beaufort-en-Santerre.

The men of the 8th Battalion were greeted with a hail of machine-gun fire coming from Hatchet Wood. Caught in the open the Winnipegs could find no cover to advance and were slowly

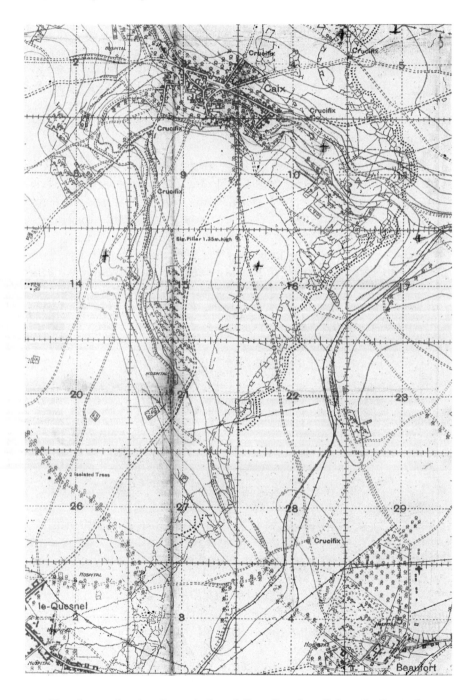

Trench map showing Outer Amiens defence line from Caix to Le Quesnel.

being wiped-out by the Germans. As had always been the Canadian trademark the situation was saved by the gallantry of individuals.

Corporal Fred Coppins[5] and four men rushed another German machine-gun post just north of Hatchet Wood that was destroying the men trapped in the open field. The fire was so heavy that all four of Coppins' men were killed in the assault, but Coppins single-handedly silenced the gun and killed or captured the crew.

In another platoon of the 8th Battalion, Lance-Corporal Alec Brereton[6] fearlessly assaulted a German machine-gun position, killed the crew and forced nine others to surrender. Brereton's actions saved many of his comrades and allowed the advance to continue. Both Coppins and Brereton were awarded the Victoria Cross for their actions on August 9th, 1918.

Even with all this courage the 8th had suffered grievously. Their C.O., Lieutenant Colonel Thomas Raddall and 65 of his officers and men are buried in Manitoba Cemetery. A further 230 were wounded.

South of the cemetery the 5th Battalion also came under heavy machine-gun fire from Warvillers. On two occasions Sergeant Raphael Zengel[7] of the 5th Battalion single-handedly eliminated German positions and continued the advance. In the fields east of Warvillers he rushed 200 metres ahead of the attack and killed or routed the enemy. Throughout the battle he scouted-out well-hidden German machine-gun nests and directed fire at them. For his courage and leadership Zengel was awarded the Victoria Cross.

By the end of the day the Canadians had pushed the Germans back 6 km and captured the villages of Warvillers, Beaufort, Vrely, Folies, Bouchoir, Rosieres and Meharicourt. Although the German defences had stiffened it was still a great victory. But the battle had reached the old 1916 battlefield, a rabbit-warren of uncharted, dilapidated trenches and dug-outs. This was a perfect, prepared defensive line for the enemy.

Return to your car and continue 2 km into Beaufort village. It was captured by the 2nd Battalion on August 9th. Turn left on the D161 to Warvillers, pass through the village on the D161

---

[5] Frederick George Coppins; born London, England, October 25, 1889; died Livermore, California, March 30, 1963.

[6] Alexander Picton Brereton; born Oak River, Manitoba, November 13; died Calgary, Alberta, June 11, 1976.

[7] Raphael Louis Zengel; born Faribault, Minnesota, USA; died Errington, British Columbia, February 22, 1977.

(Henry Norwest of the 50th (Alberta) Battalion, Canada's highest scoring sniper is buried in the churchyard at Warvillers), and continue to Rouvroy-en-Santerre. You are passing through the battlefield fought over by the 2nd, 5th, and 4th Battalions on August 9th, 1918. The 3rd Battalion captured Rouvroy village.

Pass through the village and stay on the D161 to Fouquescourt village. Once in the village follow directions north to Maucourt and Fouquescourt British Cemetery. The cemetery in 150 metres north of the village on a small side road. Drive to the cemetery and stop.

Point 7: Fouquescourt British Cemetery; the attack of the 4th Division, August 10th, 1918.

The flat farmland which surrounds you, which is so pretty and tranquil today, was the biggest obstacle facing the Canadian Corps in the Battle of Amiens. In 1916, this region was the front line, where both the French and Germans had spent countless hours digging trenches, inter-connecting dug-outs, laying barbed-wire; all the important things an Army did in the Great War. For three years it was the front line until, in 1917, the Germans, in a general withdrawal, retreated to the Hindenburg line. Since that time the trench works rotted and collapsed, but their essential purpose of providing good defensive works remained. Now they formed a formidable obstacle, more than 3 km deep, and extending the length of the Canadian attack. The rapid advance of the Canadians had brought them into the old 1916 lines. Any advance would have to be won in close combat where success would depend on individuals not battalions or divisions. There would be no more huge advances.

Over the next few days the Canadians would try to breakthrough the old lines, but the result was some of the most confused fighting in the war.

To the Generals the objective of the third day of the offensive was to continue the push. The Canadian Corps would employ the 3rd and 4th Divisions in the attack on August 10th. The 4th Division would attack from Fouquescourt north and the 32nd Imperial Division from just south of Fouquescourt to the D934.

Looking west across the flat farmland, the church spires from each of the small villages can be seen. North-west is Meharicourt, west is Rouvroy, and north are the small villages of Maucourt and

Chilly. On August 10th at 8:00 am, six battalions of the 4th Division attacked the old trench lines. Fouquescourt British Cemetery is located in the middle of the old lines. Due to the rough terrain tanks could not assist this attack. The 44th (Manitoba) and 47th (Western Ontario) Battalions led the assault across the fields in front of you. You can imagine the waves of Canadian soldiers gradually advancing until reaching the old defences; and the chatter of machine-gun fire from the German positions. Men fall but the advance slowly continues and steadily the Canadians push on. Fighting, trench by trench, the 44th captured the village and linked up with the 47th Battalion. By 6 pm the entire village was in Canadian hands. Looking east the men of the 44th Division pushed out beyond the village and dug in to await German counter-attacks. At this point in the battle the 44th realized the 32nd (Imperial or British) Division on their right was more than 1.5 km behind them and their flank was exposed. The Germans shelled the Canadian positions throughout the evening of August 10th. After midnight the Germans mounted a series of counter-attacks on the Canadian lines east and north of the village. The attacks continued until dawn but all were repulsed by the firmly entrenched men of the 44th and 47th Battalions.

Return to your car and drive back into Fouquescourt village. Continue straight through the village following the road to Parvillers-le-Quesnoy (2.5 km away). You are driving just east of, and parallel to the old Somme defences. Just south of Fouquescourt was the scene of heavy fighting by the 42nd (Black Watch of Montreal) Battalion. The action is best described in Will Birds' "Ghosts Have Warm Hands". To your left, just south of Fouquescourt was the scene of Thomas Dinesen's courageous exploits which resulted in the Danish-born member of the 42nd Battalion winning the Victoria Cross. The fighting in the old Somme defence lines was intense and only the courage and initiative of individuals and small groups kept the advance going. Dinesen's[8] actions were outstanding, in that time and time again he led assaults on German positions capturing machine-gun posts and driving the enemy back. His courage led to an advance of more than 1.5 km through the enemy positions.

---

[8] Thomas Dinesen; born Copenhagen, Denmark, August 9, 1892; died Leerbaek, Denmark, March 10, 1979.

THE 44TH MEN AT FOUQUESCOURT

The following was taken from the Official History of the 44th Canadian Infantry Battalion, entitled "Six Thousand Men" by E.S. Russenholt.

"It is ten in the morning when the 44th moves out to the attack in four waves--at 300 yards distance, with Lewis guns in front. Passing over the Meharicourt Road, the men encounter a maze of trenches and wire. These are the old Somme defences. Two full miles deep they stand, between the 44th men and their objective in the village of Fouquescourt. A heavy enemy barrage comes down--unpleasantly significant of the presence of powerful enemy reinforcements.

"Moving steadily forward, in widely extended formation, the 44th men pass through the enemy barrage; step by step, the survivors drive in the enemy outpost line--step by step, the waves fight their way through the tangled trench system. At last they are through! The leading Companies emerge upon the old No-Man's Land between the original French and German lines. Suddenly, as if by a given signal--from trenches in front, from the village of Fouquescourt, from the high ground on the right which is not being attacked--a terrific storm of machine gun fire burst upon the advancing Companies. Waves begin to lose formation. Swept by the storm of fire from front and flanks--impeded by the trenches and wire--the 44th men fall behind the barrage movement. But Company and platoon commanders continue the attack by section rushes. A determined struggle begins. Slowly, but steadily, the 44th men win ground, despite the fire concentrated upon them. Efforts to gain touch with the unit on the right yield the disquieting information that the troops on that flank have been stopped nearly a mile back.

"Tanks detailed to the 44th attack run into the deep trenches of the old Somme system and are unable to move forward. For this reason, all tanks allotted to the Tenth Brigade attack swing over to the front of the 46th battalion whose objective, Maucourt, is in open ground free of the Somme trenches.

"Thus, without the aid of the tanks, the 44th men face the grim task alone. Fighting their way forward in small parties, they secure a foothold in the old German front line. Yard by yard--with bullet, bayonet and bomb--they force their way ahead. One after another, the capture the enemy machine guns. They drive out the garrison from trench after trench, which are left littered with equipment discarded by the retiring defenders. Pressing steadily forward, at last the final line of trenches is reached. Between the Battalion and its objective in the village is an open valley; along it sweeps a stream of concentrated machine gun fire.

"In the last trenches, the 44th platoons are rallied. The S.O.S. for artillery assistance is sent up. Promptly the supporting batteries respond. Shells rain upon the village of Fouquescourt--immediately in front. Under this protective barrage the leading platoons make a determined dash for their objective--the village. The heroism displayed in this phase of the attack is beyond all praise. Capt. Neale, M.C., one of the best-known officers of the Battalion, dies--gallantly leading an attack on North Wood in the outskirts. In the same attack, Capt. J.W. Macdonald is wounded. Along walls, through houses, down narrow streets, the 44th men push on. Lieut. G.W. Matheson is killed as his men battle their way as far as Fouquescourt church. Capt. G.W. Epton is wounded twice in three attacks--but his men finally gain a footing in the village. No.3 Company, under Capt. R.C. Rowland, drives through to the far side of the village--clearing out five successive nests of machine guns. Lieut. J.W. Ferguson and the remnant of his platoon also win through to the farther edge of the village.

"Unfortunately, as the 44th platoons turn to mop up the multitude of German posts in orchards, houses and cellars, the Canadian guns (prompted by officers in the rear who are unacquainted with the forward situation) again open heavily on the village. After 20 men are hit the platoon withdraw from the forward side--but hold grimly on to the western edge of the town. They have broken the German hold on Fouquescourt--and, sheltering in gardens, cellars and ruins, they maintain their positions in the face of fire focussed upon them from all directions. Immediately the fire of the Canadian batteries is corrected, the 44th parties, led by Lieuts. Barnes and Galbraith, occupy the high ground to the right--ready to support a renewed attack on the village. Two tanks come up. The 44th platoons are assembled, and the Battalion sweeps into Fouquescourt, closely followed by the 47th. By 6 p.m. all ranks have turned in a good day's work--Fouquescourt has been cleared of enemy troops!"

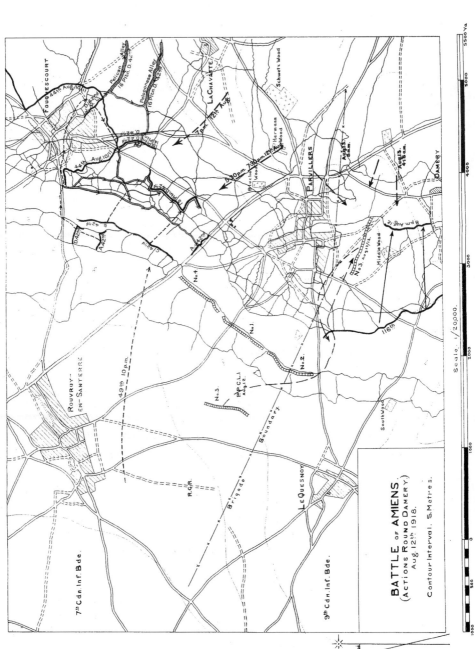

Local actions around Damery and Parvillers, 3rd Division, August 12th, 1918.

Continue to Parvillers (the road merges and becomes the D34). Drive past the D161E, 0.5 km past the village, a side road to Damery appears on your right. Turn onto the side road and stop your car.

Point 8: Parvillers; the assault of the 3rd Canadian Division, August 12th to 15th, 1918.

Looking 1 km west across the open fields south of Parvillers you can see the area fought over by the Princess Patricia's Canadian Light Infantry, Royal Canadian Regiment and the 116th Battalion. The 3rd Division was brought in on August 12th, 1918 to relieve the badly battered 32nd Imperial Division. The fighting was ferocious and the Germans threw all available reserves against the infiltrating Canadians. As with the fighting around Fouquescourt, the situation was one of confusion; of units advancing, being cut-off, retreating and advancing once again.

In one such action on the night of August 12th/13th just south of Parvillers a platoon of the PPCLI had been cut-off by a German counter-attack. The group of soldiers fought valiantly but against overwhelming odds were forced back. With the Germans on three sides and closing quickly, it was up to a few individuals to slow the Germans and allow the others to get away. Sergeant Robert Spall[9] took a Lewis gun and stood on a parapet, and fired into the advancing Germans. He inflicted heavy casualties on the attackers. Spall directed his men out of the trench and then, in a show of incredible courage once again turned a Lewis gun on the enemy. This time he had no intention of leaving his post. Sergeant Spall deliberately gave up his life so his comrades could get away.

For his bravery Sergeant Robert Spall was awarded the Victoria Cross, posthumously. The action took place just 500 metres north-west of where you now stand. Spall's body was never identified after the war and he is commemorated on the Vimy Memorial. He is most likely buried as an unknown in Bouchoir New British Cemetery.

The village of Parvillers was attacked and captured by the PPCLI again on August 14th, 1918. But as on the 13th, the Germans counter-attacked from a wood east of the village cutting-off

[9] Robert Spall; born Brentford, Middlesex, England, March 5, 1890; died Parvillers, France, August 13, 1918.

The 42nd (Black Watch Of Canada) Battalion at Parvillers,
(From the memoir "Ghosts Have Warm Hands" by Will R. Bird.).

"When it came daylight we saw we were in old grassed trenches, with many concrete emplacements about, and wide tangles of rusting barbed wire at every corner. We stood where we were a time and then had something to eat. There was no shelling. The front seemed comparatively quiet.

"It had become quite warm. We had lost Granny, and no one knew where he was. Then Major Arthur told us he was going to visit another part of the front, and to wait until he returned. The attack was not going to be made until two or three o'clock. The sergeant-major came and said nothing was definite. He had talked with some of the Border non-coms and they had told him the place was a warren of old trenches, a maze that would bewilder anyone...

"... The "original" was waiting as if he were burdened with half-wits. It was fearfully warm. Even our rifles were hot. There was machine gun fire on all sides. You could not tell, by listening, where the real front was. There was wire along every trench, lots of it, and bullets ricocheted from it. We did not see anyone and suddenly were in a deeper, wider section of trench that crossed the one we were in, making a sharp T. There we halted. The "original" seemed more nervous than any of us and said he had never seen a worse mess. There were twice as many trenches as the maps showed. He was sure every platoon was lost. He did not like where we were at all. He told me to go with Norton to the left of the deep trench and explore about one hundred yards. He and the others would go to the right.

"Norton and I went slowly. The trench sides were two feet higher than my head, covered with weeds and thistles. There were webs of black, long-barbed wire, and some wooden posts whose function we wondered about. Suddenly we heard German voices. I cautioned Norton to stand ready while I climbed up and had a look through the grass and weeds. There were five German pot helmets bobbing along about fifty yards away and they were going from our area. Just then I heard Norton give a sort of gasp and turned to witness a tableau that is vivid in my memory. Norton was about six feet three inches tall, and had not shaved for two or three days. He was holding his bayonet ready and his kilt was hitched high above his great, bony knees. In his hand, pressed against the rifle butt, was a Mills bomb. And facing him was a German, a young, white-faced fellow, a mere boy. He stood in a posture of recoil, cringing. And he was not armed!

"Crack! Norton, after sixty long seconds of staring, pulled the trigger. He declared later that he had not meant to, that his finger simply tightened involuntarily on the trigger. The rifle muzzle was not six feet from the Hun and pointed at his stomach. The lad went down as if hit by a fist and groaned frightfully. I had never heard a worse sound.

"The groaning upset Norton so much that he jumped about, dropping his bomb, and ran headlong down the trench. I dropped from my perch and dived at the bomb-but the pin had not been pulled. No other Germans were in sight, but I could hear a jabber of voices a few yards around the corner, so I pulled the bomb pin and hurled the grenade in that direction, then ran after Norton.

"He was telling the "original" what he had done as I reached them and was so excited he hardly knew what he was saying. It was his first battle and his first kill. The "original" now suggested that Coleman and I go back to a traverse about one hundred yards away and watch for Germans. He and the others would explore in the other direction. We went back to the traverse, sweat running down our faces. We opened our tunics. And a party of Huns appeared twenty yards away, walking rapidly!

"The Huns had their rifles ready, but I slashed at the trigger of mine and the bullet caught the coal-bucket helmet of the big leader, striking the earth-bank alongside them and scattering a cloud of dust. One of the Germans shot but his bullet struck the earth beside us, and then Coleman fired and brought the leader down. I shot a second time, catching a short, fat goose-stepper. Coleman shot at the third German as he turned and ran, and probably winged him, for the fellow dropped his rifle and clutched his arm as he vanished around the turn.

"We hurried back and told the "original" what had happened. He decided we had better go back a distance up the trench, so the Huns could not come at us from both sides. It was a wise move. We had not gone fifty yards before Norton, using his height, saw pot helmets bobbing along the trench toward where we had been. At the same time he saw five Germans get up on the bank and start overland, so as to cut off the corner and rush us where we were. He was so excited he climbed out at a low place to meet them, and we, not knowing what was happening, followed him. The Lewis gunners jumped back in the trench when they saw five Germans with rifles ready, but for a second or so Coleman and I stayed with Norton. We fired at the Germans and they shot at us. The distance was about seventy-five yards and neither side scored a hit. The "original" yelled at us to get down, but there was a second exchange. Three of the Germans went down and both Coleman and Norton were hit. Coleman had a bullet through his arm and Norton had one eye shot out, a horrible wound. We tied him up and Coleman led him back the way we had come, as he had lost the sight of his other eye.

"The Germans pressed us. They had jumped back into the deep trench, but they hurled "potato mashers" as if they had an abundant supply. We retreated to a corner, placing the Lewis gun in position. The "original" sent one of the gunners back to report to Major Arthur and to ask for help. We were not any great distance from him, and the major himself returned with a small party. To my great relief Doggy was with them. He had been forced to leave the trench, as a party of Germans had entered it from a sap, and he had stayed hidden for a long time before risking a return. Not finding me where I had been, he had kept going until he found Fourteen Platoon.

"The Germans tried one rush and our Lewis gun played havoc with them. They left five dead before they retreated and vanished out some sap or down into some dugout. The major said we had better make sure there were no more of the enemy in the immediate area, as he did not want Fourteen Platoon attacked from the rear. The "original" said he would take the Lewis crew and explore in the direction the Germans had run. I was to take Doggy and four of the major's party and go the opposite way. A short distance along we found a 42nd man dead in the trench, his badges gone, his pockets ransacked."

some and driving the rest back. In the attack on August 14th one of the officers of the PPCLI surrounded at Parvillers was Lieutenant John Christie, my Great-Uncle. His company managed to get away from the Germans but not before the Company Commander Vivian Drummond-Hay, MC, was killed and my uncle John wounded. John Christie was awarded the Military Cross for his role in the battle.

The RCR finally captured Parvillers on August 15th.

South of where you stand the 116th Battalion attacked across the open fields on August 12th, but were driven back. On August 15th the 116th attacked again, this time in conjunction with the 52nd (New Ontario) Battalion who attacked Damery village (250 metres directly south of where you stand). Both attacks succeeded and in the case of Damery, succeeded too easily. In fact the Germans had allowed the 52nd to take the village intending to shell it and cut them off in the village. The 52nd Battalion suspecting some form of trap had pushed east of the village. When the Germans attacked, the Canadians blasted the unsuspecting Germans. What was clear to all was that the Battle of Amiens was over. There was nothing more to be gained by fighting here.

Return to Fouquescourt and continue north through the village to Maucourt. You will pass Fouquescourt British Cemetery on your right. Maucourt is 2 km north of the cemetery. You are driving over the territory captured by the 4th Division on August 10th, 1918. The area was in front of the old Somme lines so the advance here was relatively painless. The men of the 47th and 50th (Alberta) Battalions captured the open territory and Maucourt itself was captured by the 72nd (Seaforth Highlanders of Vancouver) Battalion. Once in Maucourt turn right on the D39 and drive through Chilly (captured by the 72nd Battalion on August 10th) and stay on the road to Hallu. Stop just outside Hallu.

Like the fighting in the 3rd Divisions' sector the Germans were not giving up without a fight, and it was here that the 78th Battalion, following through the 72nd, ran into stiff resistance. As the attack faltered in the face of heavy fire Lieutenant James Tait[10] led his men forward but a concealed machine-gun once again held up

---

[10] James Edward Tait; born Greenbrae, Scotland, May 27, 1886; died Chilly, France, August 11, 1918.

the advance. Tait ran forward and single-handedly put the gun out of action. His men followed him and in a short fight captured 12 machine-guns and 20 prisoners. The 78th Battalion had succeeded in capturing Hallu. Later James Tait was mortally wounded by the explosion of a German shell. He died shortly afterwards. Hallu was evacuated the next day and the Canadians withdrew to a position between Hallu and Chilly. James Tait was awarded the Victoria Cross posthumously for his courageous actions on August 10th and 11th, 1918. After the war his body was never identified and he is commemorated by a special headstone in Fouquescourt British Cemetery, superscribed "Believed to be buried in this cemetery".

Turn around and return to Chilly on the D39. Continue through Maucourt on the D39 to Meharicourt. You are driving over the ground captured by the 72nd and 46th (Saskatchewan) Battalions on August 10th, 1918. Once the outskirts of Meharicourt are reached you are driving over the territory captured by the 2nd Division's 22nd (Canadian-francais) Battalion on August 9th. In the centre of the village the D39 meets the D161 and drive south out of the village (turn right to visit the grave of Andrew Mynarski, VC, in Meharicourt Communal Cemetery).

Just south of the village take the small unnumbered road to Vrely, 2.5 km away.

It was across these fields between Vrely and Meharicourt the 22nd Battalion advanced on August 9th. On the outskirts of Meharicourt their attack was held up by a German machine-gun. Lieutenant Jean Brillant[11] attacked the position killing two Germans and capturing the gun. Later he led an attack which resulted in the capture of 150 Germans and 15 machine-guns. Unfortunately Brillant received a second wound. Undeterred he again led a charge, this time capturing a German field piece and received a third and fatal wound in this action. Brillant was evacuated to a Casualty Clearing Station at Dury, south of Amiens, where he died of his wounds. After the war the cemetery at Dury was removed and the burials concentrated at the Villers Bretonneux Military Cemetery. He is buried in Plot VI A, Row B, Grave 20.

---

[11] Jean Brillant; born Assametquaghan, Quebec, March 15, 1890; died Dury, France, August 10, 1918.

The Grave of Andy Mynarski, VC.

Although this book deals with the exploits of the Canadians in the First World War, there is a grave from the Second World War that should be visited. At the back of the Communal Cemetery in the village of Meharicourt (3 km south-east of Rosieres, on the D39E) to Fouquescourt, are buried 41 Second World War airmen. Amongst the burials is Pilot Officer Andrew Mynarski, of Winnipeg. Mynarski's

(PHOTO: NORM CHRISTIE)

Lancaster bomber was on a night raid on the French transport centre of Cambrai when it was attacked and set on fire by a German night fighter. As the crew bailed out Mynarski, the mid-gunner, noticed the tail-gunner was trapped in the rear turret. Although the Lancaster was engulfed in flames, Mynarski stayed behind, valiantly trying to free the trapped gunner. Finally with his clothing and parachute afire he had to give up and in a sad parting gesture, came to attention, saluted his friend and bailed out. The flaming Lancaster continued its descent until it crashed south of Arras, 40 km away. Miraculously the tail-gunner survived the crash and was taken prisoner. After the war Mynarski was awarded the Victoria Cross for his courageous act. Sadly Andy Mynarski was so badly burned that he died in German hands, shortly afterwards. His body could not be identified due to the burns until 1946.

Andrew Charles Mynarski was 27.

Continue on the road to Vrely, turning left into the village and then right on a small unnumbered road to Caix (4 km). Once again you are driving through the August 9th battlefield. This is the valley of the Luce River. Continue onto Caix, captured by the 7th (British Columbia) and the 10th (Alberta) Battalions on August 8th. The D76 road merges with the D28 just west of the village. Follow the D28 into Caix. The D28 forks outside of the western edge of the village, keep left following the D76 to Cayeux-en-Santerre (3.5 km) in the river valley. This area was captured by British cavalry on August 8th. At Cayeux continue on the small road to Ignaucourt (2 km) (captured by the 2nd (Eastern Ontario) Battalion on August 8th, 1918). The D76 crosses the Luce River at this point and continue to follow the D76 through Aubercourt (2 km). In 1 km the D76 meets the D23 (this is the turn off leading from Point 1 to Point 2). Turn right and after 250 metres turn right again on the D42. There should also be a signpost to Toronto Cemetery. Follow the D42 for 300 metres until a small dirt road forks to the left. Take the small dirt road. Toronto Cemetery is 1 km farther on. You may have to leave the car and walk to the cemetery. You can see the vestiges of German dugouts in the side of the sunken road. They would have led to the German front lines. When you reach the cemetery stop.

Point 9: Toronto Cemetery; the attack of the 1st Canadian Division, August 8th, 1918.

The view from this beautiful cemetery in many ways encompasses the first phase of the Battle of Amiens. The wood north of you is Morgemont Wood captured by the 14th (Royal Montreal Regiment), and the 13th Battalion. The 3rd (Toronto Regiment) Battalion leap frogged the 13th Battalion and advanced 4 km across these fields and captured 450 prisoners. The Regiment suffered 200 casualties including 40 dead.

It is interesting to reflect on the Battle of Amiens from this beautiful vantage point. The Canadian casualties for August 8th, 1918 were 3,868 including 1,036 killed. They captured 5,033 Germans but they had shattered any hope for victory that the Germans had. It was certainly "The Black day of the German Army."

By the end of the Battle the Canadians had suffered 11,822 killed or wounded, captured more than 9,000 Germans, 1,000 machine-guns and penetrated more than 22 km into German

The 4th Canadian Infantry Battalion, August 8th, 1918,

(From the memoir, "Only This, A War Retrospect" by James H. Pedley.).

"We are not yet quite into the mist, although the air is heavier and a smell of burning hangs around. Forty yards ahead the line of Fritz's barrage can now be made out, a series of explosions, flying earth and timber and thick puffs of black smoke. It would be far more formidable had not our surprise barrage put so many of his guns out of action. Still it is no joke to pass through this curtain of bursting shells...... We pass the enemy front line, and his supports. Dead and wounded lie thick here, mostly Germans, and the trenches are badly torn by the shelling. One notices the stores of bombs and S.A.A., and the biscuit tins and bits of clothing; just like a trench of our own might look. Last night these fellows took post without a thought of the disaster that was to wipe them out and open the way to the Rhine. There are more prisoners now, but the mist has got so thick we cannot see them until they are right on top of us. No stopping for souvenirs. We point to the rear and Fritz runs along contentedly enough. He has had his bellyful of war. But the mist presently grows so thick that nothing can be seen at a distance of more than ten feet or so...

"... The ground improved as we advanced up the valley. The Luce lay below us, on our right. Vic Collins and Lunt had crossed it with their platoons and were not in sight, for our company straddled the stream. Wattam and I plugged along, now over pleasant meadow land, until we came to a road at right angles to our advance. At the far edge of the road the ground rose four or five feet abruptly and you could not see what was beyond...

"... Vern's men and mine are up and off. There is a bit of bush to cross, then an open field, then a road, and at the other side of the road, another ditch. It is up and down, up and down, quick, short rushes ss Infantry Training directs. Bullets are clipping the grass in the field. The rattle of the machine-guns sounds close as on the rifle ranges.

"I am running neck and neck with Private Moreau, No. 2 on the Lewis-gun. He carries a wallet filled with spare parts for the gun; also two panniers of ammunition besides his revolver and web equipment. It is too much for him to run far with.

"Here, give me this," I shout, reaching for the panniers of S.A.A. slung on his shoulder. He misunderstands me, thinks I am hit, reaches to hold me up as we run forward together. "No, I'm all right," I yell, and shift the panniers to my shoulder. He is grateful, and smiles a moment then we are down together in the ditch.

"One man yet to come. He is back across the road. One bound will bring him into the little furrow that shelters us. Yes, but a bullet is quicker than a man. The man jumps up, there is a sharper crack as his skull is cloven, he spins around on his toes and falls heavily. It is Private Dahmer. One man less to our garrison.

"God! how the bullets crack, just above our heads! they break the twigs all around, they thud into the little bank of earth. Cautiously I move my head and look to each side of me. Moreau is on my left, and beyond him is Proctor with the Lewis-gun. The gun has jammed; he is working feverishly with it. On my right is Secord and a couple of others. Further along still Armstrong shepherds the remnants of his dozen. We are at the very base of the hill, which is not very high, but the slope is steep. Fritz is on top of us.

"Where is he? Get the guns trained on him, make it hot for him up there! Just as hot as he is making it for us. No one else will push him off this bit of hill. It is up to us. Cautiously Moreau and I raise our heads a foot apart until our eyes can see through the long grass. But we do not have time to see anything.

"Crack! Moreau is hit. He falls back, and I with him, my arm around him. My hand is wet with blood that spurts from his breast. What a flow of blood, a fountain of blood! Moreau gasps and chokes three or four times, his whole body heaving, then stiffens in a final convulsion and collapses. It is all a matter of a few seconds. The corpse is heavy and I push it from me.

"Number One has looked up from the gun and I shake my head to signify it is all over with poor Moreau. There is a sudden moisture in Number One's eyes. Someone crawls snakelike along the ditch and detaches the spare-parts wallet from Moreau's neck. It is Number Three on the gun taking his promotion.

"The gun itself is still jammed. I have no heart to poke my head out of the friendly cover of a few inches of earth. But see what is happening on my right. Who is it that kneels upright, exposed from the waist up, rifle to shoulder firing coolly and steadily? His right arm moves back and forward ejecting and thrusting in the cartridges--it is a machine, not an arm. There is a fierce proud look on the face leaning close to the rifle-butt. Is this Secord, the great lubber who did pack drills for his slacking at Cambligneul? Certainly not. Rubbish!

"Why doesn't he get hit? Is Secord a god, that he can live in that tornado of lead? See, he has emptied the magazine, plucked another clip of full rounds from his pouch, loaded with a sure hand. He is firing again. This is your moment, Private Secord, and by God, you are using it well!"

Canadians resting in shell hole made by our artillery. Battle of Amiens. August, 1918.

(PUBLIC ARCHIVES OF CANADA PA-2859)

occupied land. For Canada there was no time to celebrate, by August 20th they were moving north to engage the Germans at Arras and at the Drocourt-Queant line. It was to be their greatest battle and their greatest victory. Then again the men of the Canadian Corps would strike at the Canal-du-Nord and Cambrai and again at Valenciennes. In fact they would continue striking until the war ended on November 11th, 1918 and the last strike at Mons was delivered by the Canadians.

The "Last Hundred Days" proved to all the efficiency, and power of the Canadian Corps. They won a sense of pride, based on courage and success, unequalled in Canadian history. But the cost.... In the last three months of the war 11,882 Canadians were killed. One in five of all Canadian deaths in the First World War happened in the "Last Hundred Days". Perhaps the saddest part is that these sacrifices are forgotten. The men who lie in these cemeteries, and their families, who waited anxiously at home, do not seem to matter. There is a real tragedy in this.

Return to your car and go back to the D23. Turn right on the D23 to Villers Bretonneux. When you reach the N29-E44 at Villers Bretonneux turn left to return to Amiens or turn right to return to the A1-E15, and to Arras.

CEMETERIES AND MEMORIALS

Amiens was the first of three major victories for the Canadian Corps in the final months of the war. The impressive gains made in the battles were not only a great achievement, but also allowed for the dead to be properly buried by the Corps Burial Parties. Consequently, the majority of the dead received a known and honoured grave. There were few unidentified remains.

Of the 4,000 Canadians who died in the Battle of Amiens, more than 90% lie in the beautiful cemeteries that dot the picturesque Santerre plain and Luce River Valley. Those who died of their wounds are buried further afield, near the great hospital centres at Rouen and Etaples.

The Missing, who have no known grave, are commemorated on the Vimy Memorial, north of Arras. The majority of the missing were killed in the later phases of the battle, during the fighting in the old 1916 trenches. Amongst those whose graves were never identified was Sergeant Robert Spall of the P.P.C.L.I. Spall won the Victoria Cross on August 13th, 1918 when he stopped a Ger-

All that remains of Sergeant Robert Spall, VC; his name is engraved on the Vimy Memorial

(PHOTO: NORM CHRISTIE)

man counter-attack with a Lewis gun. He was killed in the action. The Vimy Memorial also commemorates the majority of Canadians in the cavalry and motor machine-guns killed in the March retreat. Nearly all the dead of the Royal Canadian Dragoons, Fort Garry Horse, Lord Strathcona's Horse, the Borden, Yukon and Eaton Motor Machine-Gun Batteries are commemorated at Vimy. All were killed between March 21st and April 4th, 1918.

The Canadian Cemeteries of Amiens are amongst the most beautiful in France. Most are small, left as they were made by the burial parties. They have been nicely landscaped and the wooden crosses have been replaced by Portland headstones. They sit in the rolling countryside, almost appearing as a natural feature. But like the cemeteries from the Canadian Battles at Cambrai and Arras, they receive few visitors. The lack of notice of the sacrifice of these brave men seems to deepen the tragedy of their loss.

LEST WE FORGET.

LONGEAU BRITISH CEMETERY

The Cemetery is located on the south-east side of Amiens on the road to Roye (D934).

It was originally made in 1918 and used by the Canadians during the Battle of Amiens. After the war, 36 graves were concentrated into it. It now contains 202 Commonwealth burials, including 66 Canadian soldiers (1 unknown).

Lieutenant-Colonel Elmer Jones, the Commanding Officer of the 21st (Eastern Ontario) Battalion is buried in Plot III, Row B, Grave 1. He was killed August 8th, 1918, near Marcelcave. He was 44.

Lieutenant-Colonel Bartlett McLennan, Commanding Officer of the 42nd (Royal Highlanders of Canada) Battalion is buried in Plot II, Row D, Grave 7. He was killed by a sniper, August 3rd, 1918, when reconnoitring the new lines. McLennan was 49.

BOVES EAST COMMUNAL CEMETERY

Boves is a village 8 km south-east of Amiens, just south of the Roye road. The Cemetery is located in the north of the village. It contains 15 Commonwealth burials, including 4 Canadians.

BOVES WEST COMMUNAL CEMETERY EXTENSION

The cemetery is located in the western part of the village. It was made by fighting units in August, 1918, and was enlarged by the concentration of 32 graves after the war. The cemetery now contains 91 graves, including 48 Canadians. The majority of the Canadians buried here died of wounds received in the later stages of the battle, August 14th to 20th.

There is one Canadian soldier buried in BOVES WEST COMMUNAL CEMETERY.

HOURGES ORCHARD CEMETERY, Domart-sur-la-Luce.

Domart-sur-la-Luce is a village 15 km south-east of Amiens on the main road to Roye (D934), The cemetery is located just north of the road.

The cemetery was made by the Canadian Corps Burial Officer in August 1918. It contains 126 Commonwealth burials, including 120 Canadians (3 unidentified). The graves are predominantly 3rd Division (45 men of the 43rd Battalion and 39 of the 116th Battalion) soldiers killed August 8th, 1918. Each headstone marks the graves of two soldiers, indicating a trench burial. This is typical of the Amiens battlefield cemeteries.

DEMUIN BRITISH CEMETERY

Demuin is a small village located in the valley of the Luce river 18 km east of Amiens. The Cemetery was made by the Canadian Corps Burial Officer in August, 1918. It contains the graves of 42 Commonwealth soldiers, including 40 Canadians. The burials are men of the 3rd Brigade (13th and 16th Battalions), 1st Canadian Division, killed August 8th, 1918.

TORONTO CEMETERY, Demuin.

Toronto Cemetery is located in open fields, 2 km north of Demuin village. The cemetery was started in August, 1918 and contains the graves of 97 Commonwealth soldiers, including 74 Canadians (4 unidentified).

The burials are predominantly men of the 1st Canadian Division, in particular 29 soldiers of the 3rd (Toronto Regiment) Battalion, from whom the cemetery gets its name. The view from the cemetery captures the feel of the Battle of Amiens. The road leading into the cemetery is difficult, and a visit will require a walk of roughly 500 metres.

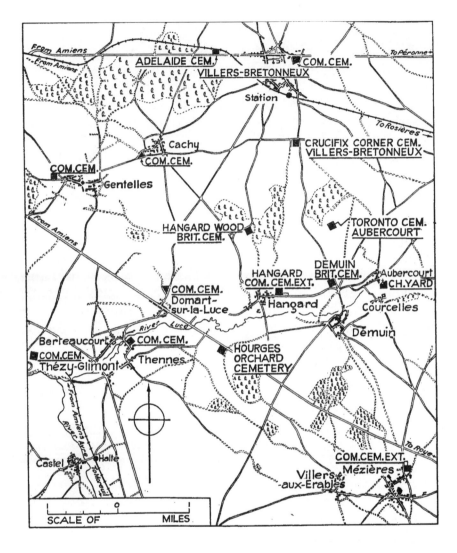

Cemetery locations - Amiens Battlefield
(COMMONWEALTH WAR GRAVES COMMISSION)

HANGARD WOOD BRITISH CEMETERY

Hangard is a small village located in the valley of the Luce river, 18 km east of Amiens. The cemetery is located 2 km north of the village, between two woods, Hangard Wood, East and West. It was started by the Canadian Corps Burial Officer in August 1918. The original cemetery was enlarged by 22 concentrations from the battlefields, ranging as far north as the Somme. It now contains 141 Commonwealth graves, including 61 Canadians (2 unidentified).

The Canadian burials are men of the 1st Division (13th and 16th Battalions) killed August 8th, 1918 in the initial assault. Amongst the burials is Private John Bernard Croak, VC, of the 13th (Black Watch) Battalion. A Newfoundlander, Croak won his Victoria Cross posthumously, for attacking and capturing several German machine-guns. John Croak is buried in Plot I, Row A, Grave 9. He was 24.

Buried in Plot I, Row A, Grave 1 is Captain Norman McLeod MacLean, also of the 13th Battalion. MacLean was one of 3 brothers from Inverness, Scotland killed in the war.

HANGARD COMMUNAL CEMETERY EXTENSION

The Communal Cemetery is located east of the village. It was started by the Canadian Corps Burial Officer in August 1918 with the burial of 51 Canadians in Plot I. After the war, more than 500 graves were brought in from the surrounding battlefields. It now contains the graves of 555 Commonwealth soldiers, of which 294

Canadian and German wounded at 10th Field Ambulance Dressing Station. Hangard. Battle of Amiens. August, 1918.

(PUBLIC ARCHIVES OF CANADA-PAC PA2864)

are unidentified. Amongst the burials are 72 Canadians (21 unidentified).

The concentrations included the graves of 10 Canadian Caval-rymen killed at Moreuil Wood, as well as many men of the 1st, 3rd and 4th Divisions killed east of Demuin.

BEAUCOURT BRITISH CEMETERY

Beaucourt-en-Santerre is a small village located 26 km east of Amiens and 2 km north of the road to Roye (D934). The ceme-tery was started by the Canadian Corps Burial Officer in August 1918. It contains the graves of 77 Canadian soldiers (one is uniden-tified). The burials are predominantly the 4th Division (particularly the 102nd, 54th and 75th Battalions) killed near Le Quesnel, August 8th-9th, 1918. The cemetery is located east of the village on a hillock on the road to Le Quesnel. It is one of the most beautiful in France.

MEZIERES COMMUNAL CEMETERY EXTENSION

Mezieres is a village 19 km south-east of Amiens on the road to Roye (D934). The cemetery is north of the village, adjoining the local cemetery. It was started by the Canadian Corps Burial Officer in August 1918 and enlarged by the concentration of 107 burials from the surrounding battlefields. The cemetery contains 37 Canadians, including one unidentified. Sixty-one of the 95 British graves are unidentified. They were soldiers killed in the March Retreat.

WOOD CEMETERY, Marcelcave.

Marcelcave is a small village 16 km east of Amiens and 10 km north of the main road to Roye (D934). Wood Cemetery is 2 km south-east of the village. It is 200 metres off the road to Ignaucourt.

The cemetery was made by the Canadian Corps Burial Officer in August 1918. It contains the graves of 50 Commonwealth sol-diers. Forty-one are Canadians (2 unidentified). They are principally men of the 2nd Division killed August 8th-9th, 1918.

CRUCIFIX CORNER CEMETERY, Villers-Bretonneux.

Villers-Bretonneux is a large village 10 km east of Amiens. The cemetery is located 2 km south of the village on the road to Demuin (D23).

It was started by the Canadian Corps Burial Officer in August

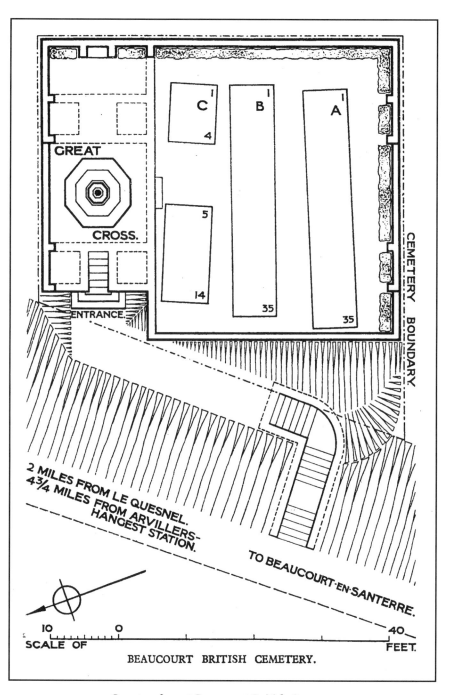

Cemetery layout Beaucourt British Cemetery

1918 and enlarged after the war. It now contains 656 Common-wealth burials including 76 Canadians (6 unidentified). Most of the Canadian burials are men of the 2nd Division killed in the initial assault August 8th, 1918. They are buried in Plot I.

The cemetery also contain the graves of 293 Australians, 142 French (including many Moroccan graves) and 2 Russian soldiers.

CAIX BRITISH CEMETERY

Caix is a village 22 km east of Amiens and 7 km north of the main road to Roye (D934). The cemetery is south-east of the village.

It was made after the war by the concentration of small cemeteries and isolated graves from the surrounding battlefields. It now contains the graves of 360 Commonwealth soldiers, including 218 Canadians. Twenty-one Canadian graves are unknown. Soldiers from all four Canadian Divisions and the Canadian Cavalry Brigade are buried in the cemetery. Amongst the burials is Lieutenant Bill Amsden of the 4th (Central Ontario) Battalion. He was the good friend of James Pedley, the author of "Only This". Pedley's book is one of the best, most detailed memoirs, and his descriptions of his friends and of the Battle of Amiens are exceptional. Amsden is buried in Plot I, Row G, Grave 3.

In addition to the Canadians graves, their are 30 troopers of the British Cavalry buried here. Several were members of the 17th Lancers and their headstones are engraved with the fearsome skull and crossbones. Six tank crew are interred in Caix.

Caix German Cemetery is just west of the cemetery. It contains 1,264 German burials.

HILLSIDE CEMETERY, Le Quesnel.

Le Quesnel is a small village on the main road to Roye (D934), 20 km east of Amiens.

Hillside Cemetery is 3 km north of the village on the road to Caix. It was made by the Canadian Corps Burial Officer in August 1918 and contains 108 Commonwealth burial, including 101 Canadians (3 unidentified).

The cemetery contains predominantly 4th Division burials, including 23 men of the 78th (Winnipeg Grenadiers) Battalion killed in a German air raid, August 24th, 1918.

Buried in Plot II, Row B, Grave 3, is Lieutenant Hedley Goodyear of the 102nd (Central Ontario) Battalion. Goodyear was one of six family members to serve in the war. Hailing from Grand Falls, NFLD, the children of Louisa and Josiah Goodyear paid dearly for their parents' loyalty to the Empire. Two sons, Raymond and Stanley were killed in action fighting with the Newfoundland Regiment. Two other brothers were wounded serving with the same Regiment, and their daughter Kate was a nursing sister. Hedley was shot through the head by a German sniper when he made the fatal error of lighting a cigarette in the front line trenches at night. He was 31.

This beautiful cemetery is built into a sloping ridge overlooking the Caix to Le Quesnel road.

LE QUESNEL COMMUNAL CEMETERY EXTENSION

Le Quesnel is a village 20 km east of Amiens in the D934. The cemetery is in the north of the village adjourning the Communal Cemetery.

It was made by the Canadian Corps Burial Officer in August 1918. It contains the graves of 61 Commonwealth soldiers, including 54 Canadians (5 unidentified). The majority of the burials are men of the 1st Division, killed August 9th, 1918.

The cemetery was re-opened during the Second World War for the burial of seven RAF servicemen killed accidentally in 1939-40.

MANITOBA CEMETERY, Caix.

Manitoba Cemetery is 3 km south of Caix on the road to Beaufort-en-Santerre. It is visible across the open fields from Hillside Cemetery. It was made by the Canadian Corps Burial Officer in August 1918.

The majority of the burials are men of the 5th, 8th and 14th Battalions, killed August 9th, 1918 in the attack on Warvillers and Hatchet Wood.

The 8th Battalion suffered heavily in the action. Sixty-six of their dead are buried here, including their Commanding Officer, Lieutenant-Colonel Thomas Raddall (Row A, Grave 4) and seven of his officers. The 8th Battalion won two Victoria Crosses in the action. The cemetery takes its name from the home province of the 8th Battalion.

ROSIERES COMMUNAL CEMETERY EXTENSION

Rosieres-en-Santerre is a village 24 km east of Amiens. The cemetery is in the northern part of the village. It was started by the Canadian Corps Burial Officer in August 1918 (Plot I, Rows A-E) and enlarged after the war. The extension now contains 434 Commonwealth burials including 156 Canadians. The Canadians buried here are principally 2nd Division killed in the taking of the village and soldiers killed or died of wounds from later in the battle.

Amongst the 156 Canadian burials is the grave of Private Arthur Hackney of the 29th (British Columbia) Battalion. Hackney was killed on August 9th, 1918, when the 29th captured Rosieres. He had served in the Boer War (1899-1902), and with the New Zealand Expeditionary Force (NZEF) earlier in the war, when he was wounded and lost the sight in one eye. Somehow, after discharge from the NZEF he enlisted at Vancouver, and returned to France. How the man, blind in one eye, passed the medical examination is unknown. Arthur Hackney is buried in Plot I, Row B, Grave 26. He was 36.

Amiens Front - Rosieres. April and May 1919.

(PUBLIC ARCHIVES OF CANADA-PAC PA4536)

VRELY COMMUNAL CEMETERY EXTENSION

Vrely is a small village 3 km south of Rosieres. The cemetery is located at the north-west end of the village. It was made by the Canadian Corps Burial Officer in August 1918 and contains the graves of 43 Commonwealth soldiers, including 39 Canadians (4 unidentified). The Canadians buried here are 2nd Division, mostly 22nd, 24th, 25th and 26th Battalions, killed August 9th, 1918 in the taking of the village.

WARVILLERS CHURCHYARD EXTENSION

Warvillers is a village located 5 km south of Rosieres. The cemetery is south of the church, and is reached through a gate at the back of the civil cemetery. It was made by the Canadian Corps in August 1918. It contains 47 Commonwealth burials, including 35 Canadians (1 unidentified).

Henry "Duckie" Norwest, of the 50th Battalion, the most famous Canadian sniper of the war, is buried in Row A, Grave 30. Norwest, a Canadian Indian from Sacred Heart, Alberta had 117 confirmed "hits" before being "hit" himself on August 18th, 1918.

FOUQUESCOURT BRITISH CEMETERY

Fouquescourt is a village 30 km east of Amiens and 8 km southeast of Rosieres. The cemetery is north of the village in the road to Maucourt. It was made after the war by the concentration of several small cemeteries from the surrounding battlefields. The cemetery now contains 373 Commonwealth burials including 137 Canadians (54 are unknown).

The Canadians buried here are predominantly 4th Division killed August 10th, 1918 in the capture of Fouquescourt and in the ensuing fighting, and 3rd Division men killed in the confused fighting in the warren of old trenches from the 1916 battlefields.

The unknowns are almost all men of the 4th Division particularly 47th, 38th, 50th, and 78th Battalions. Fouquescourt has the highest percentage of Canadian unknowns (39%) of any 1918 cemetery.

Believed to be buried amongst the unknowns in Lieutenant James Tait, VC, of the 78th Battalion. Tait won his Victoria Cross posthumously for attacking a hidden German machine-gun which was holding up the advance at Hallu. His "Special Memorial" is located at the north-west end of the cemetery.

BOUCHOIR NEW BRITISH CEMETERY

Bouchoir is a village on the main Roye road (D949), 26 km south-east of Amiens. The cemetery is located 3 km south-east of the village, just north of the main road.

The cemetery was made after the war by the concentration of small cemeteries and isolated graves from the surrounding battle-fields. It now contains 758 Commonwealth graves, including 514 Canadians (23 are unknown).

The Canadian graves reflect the fighting in the old 1916 trench lines around Parvillers and Damery, and are predominantly men of the 3rd Division. It is probable the grave of Sergeant Robert Spall, VC, of the PPCLI, is one of the unknowns buried in Bouchoir.

Major Vivian Drummond-Hay, MC, also of the PPCLI, is buried in Plot III, Row A, Grave 4. He was killed on August 14th, 1918 at Parvillers, and died in the arms of my Great-Uncle John. His brother Eric, an officer in the 16th (Canadian Scottish) Battalion, was killed two weeks later in the attack on the Drocourt Queant line. They were the sons of Mr E. Drummond-Hay of Kitscoty, Alberta. They were 23 and 20 years old respectively.

The majority the Canadian dead from the Battle of Amiens lie in the small cemeteries mentioned above. It was the Canadian way. The Australians decided to do it differently and their many little cemeteries were concentrated to larger sites. In many cases some Canadian graves were also concentrated, and they lie in the larger Australian cemeteries, some distance from where they fell. The main cemeteries to which the Canadians were concentrated are listed below.

VILLERS-BRETONNEUX MILITARY CEMETERY

Villers-Bretonneux is a town 20 km east of Amiens in the main road from Amiens to St. Quentin (N29 E44). The cemetery is located 2 km north of the town on the road to Corbie.

It is the site of Australia's National Memorial, their equivalent of Vimy. A large Memorial Tower centres the panels listing the names of 11,000 Australians who were killed in France and have no known grave. A tremendous view of the Amiens battlefield can be seen from the top of the Tower. A bronze Orientation table helps clarify the beautiful, undulating farmland that surrounds the Memorial.

The cemetery was made after the war from concentration of smaller cemeteries from the battlefields. It now contains 2,135

Commonwealth graves, including; 772 Australians and 266 Canadians (15 are unidentified).

One hundred and ninety-five Canadian graves were brought in from Dury Hospital Military Cemetery (south of Amiens) and 53 from Midway Cemetery, Marcelcave from the Amiens battlefield.

Lieutenant Jean Brillant, VC, MC, of the 22nd Battalion is buried in Plot VIA, Row B, Grave 20. Brillant won his Victoria Cross, posthumously, for exceptional bravery near Meharicourt, during the Battle of Amiens.

HEATH CEMETERY, Harbonnieres.

Harbonnieres is a village 20 km east of Amiens, just south of the main road to St. Quentin (N29-44). The cemetery is located in the main road to St. Quentin, North of the village. It was made after the war and contains 1,493 Commonwealth graves; including 985 Australians and 9 Canadians (2 are unidentified).

ADELAIDE CEMETERY, Villers-Bretonneux.

Villers-Bretonneux is a town on the main road from Amiens to St. Quentin (N29-E44), 10 km east of Amiens. The cemetery is located 2 km west of the town, on the main road. It contains 954

View from the tower at the Australian National Memorial, Villers Bretonneux.

(PHOTO: NORM CHRISTIE)

Commonwealth graves, including; 519 Australians and 22 Canadians (including 3 unidentified).

In 1993 the grave of an Unknown Australian soldier was exhumed from Adelaide Cemetery and removed to the Australian War Memorial, Canberra, Australia, where he was re-buried as Australia's "Unknown Soldier." A specially inscribed headstone marks the place where he had rested for 75 years. To date Canada has not followed suit.

CERISY-GAILLY MILITARY CEMETERY

Cerisy-Gailly is a village on the south side of the Somme river, 20 km east of Amiens. It is reached by a small road running east from Corbie. The cemetery is on the west side of the village. It contains the graves of 745 Commonwealth soldiers, including 65 Canadians (5 are unidentified).

Fifty-six of the Canadian graves came from Beaufort British Cemetery near Fouquescourt. Amongst the burials is Captain David McAndie of the 10th (Alberta) Battalion. McAndie was awarded three awards for bravery, two as an enlisted man. He won his Military Medal during the Battle of Vimy Ridge, and the Distinguished Conduct Medal for exceptional bravery at the Somme. After he was commissioned he won the Military Cross on the first day of the Amiens attack. McAndie was killed in action near Damery August 15th, 1918. He was 31. Captain David McAndie, MC, DCM, MM, is buried in Plot II, Row D, Grave 23. Ironically, buried in Grave 20 is Private Wilson Norman Ling of the 2nd (Eastern Ontario) Battalion. Ling has the dubious honour of being the last Canadian soldier executed for desertion in the war[12]. He was shot August 12th, 1918. Both were originally buried at Beaufort. Clearly, in death all men are equal.

ROYE NEW BRITISH CEMETERY

Roye is a town in the Department of the Somme, 40 km from Amiens. The cemetery is located 2 km south-east of the town on the road to Noyon (D 934).

The cemetery was made after the war and now contains the graves of 534 Commonwealth soldiers, of which 65 are Canadian (15 are unidentified).

---

[12] See "For Freedom And Honour?" by A. B. Godefroy. CEF BOOKS 1998

The Canadian dead belong to the 3rd Division, 43rd (Cameron Highlanders of Winnipeg) and 52nd (Northern Ontario) Battalions, killed August 14th-16th, 1918 in the fighting around Damery and Fresnoy-les-Roye. One of the officers of the 52nd Battalion, killed in the action, was Lieutenant Burpee Clair Churchill. Churchill was from Waialua, Oahu, Hawaiian Islands. Two other 52nd officers; Edward L. Abbott and William Johnstone, both won the Military Cross twice in the war. Their good luck ran out at Damery.

HOSPITAL CENTRES

CROUY BRITISH CEMETERY

Crouy is a village on the south side of the Somme River, 18 km west of Amiens on the D3 to Abbeville. The cemetery is located 2 km south of the village on the small road to Cavillon (D95).

During the German March Offensive and the Battle of Amiens the seriously wounded were evacuated to the Casualty Clearing Station located at Crouy. The cemetery contains 738 Commonwealth dead including 179 Canadians. The dead are from all units of the Canadian Corps.

Corporal Harry Miner, VC, of the 58th (Central Ontario) Battalion is buried in Plot V, Row B, Grave 11.

ST. SEVER CEMETERY AND EXTENSION, ROUEN

Rouen was a main Headquarters hospital centre throughout the war. The dead were buried at St. Sever Cemetery, 3 km south of the Rouen Cathedral.

The cemetery and extension contains 11,376 Commonwealth burials including 443 Canadians. The Canadian burials reflect every major and minor action the Canadians were involved in from 1915 to the Battle of Amiens.

The First Canadian Army liberated Rouen from German Occupation in 1944.

THE LLANDOVERY CASTLE

The sinking of the Llandovery Castle by the U-boat 86 on the evening of June 27th, 1918 was one of the more infamous "outrages" committed by the "Hun" in the War. To make this an even bigger propaganda opportunity, the machine-gunning of 14 Canadian Nursing Sisters, as their lifeboat was sucked into the vortex of the sinking ship, became a call for Revenge. The Canadian attack during the Battle of Amiens, August 8th, 1918 was known as the "Llandovery Castle" operations.

The S.S. Llandovery Castle was appropriated by the British Government in 1915. It became a hospital ship in September 1917 and taken over by the Canadian Army Medical Corps in March 1918. She had made 4 voyages to Halifax with wounded and was returning, with a crew of 164 and staff of 94 CAMC personnel, to Liverpool when she was attacked without warning even though she was clearly displaying her illuminated Red Cross.

Around 9:30 pm, 116 miles south-west of the Fastnet, U-86, under the command of Lieutenant Patzig, torpedoed the vessel. Patzig was well aware it was a hospital ship he was attacking. He also knew it was against orders. The torpedo struck amidship on the port side and the ship sank in 10 minutes. Evacuation had proceeded without panic and the Nursing Sisters and the Ship's Captain all made off the vessel. The H.M.H.S. Llandovery Castle was well-equipped with lifeboats and 5 boats got away. Two of the lifeboats capsized, leaving only 3 afloat.

The Captain's boat was hailed by the U-86 and Captain Sylvester was taken aboard the submarine and questioned by Patzig. Patzig was sure the Llandovery Castle was carrying munitions and American Airmen. Assured that this was not the case he was returned to his lifeboat. After some delay the U-boat returned and questioned several others about the ship's cargo. Each time the men were returned to the lifeboat, finally sailing beyond visual range. After a time they heard firing and saw flashes of explosions.

On the morning of June 29th, 1918 the Captain's lifeboat and it's 24 occupants were discovered by a British Destroyer. Searches of the area did not find the other 2 lifeboats and on July 1 the search was called off. Now the 146 crew members and 88 CAMC staff, including 14 Nursing Sisters, were listed as missing, presumed drowned.

*The grave of Captain W.J.
Enright, CAMC, in Les Baraques
Military Cemetery on the southern
outskirts of Calais. The date of
death·on the tombstone reads 14
October, 1918. In fact, Captain
Enright drowned when his Hospital Ship, the Llandovery Castle
was sunk by a German U-boat on
27th June 1918, 116 miles west
of the Fastnet. Two hundred and
thirty-four of the 258 on board
perished, including fourteen
Canadian Nursing Sisters, and
Captain Enright. His body was
recovered and honoured with a
burial at sea. Three and a half
months later, his body washed
ashore at Calais, where he was
given his final burial.*

There was considerable panic by the authorities, but it wasn't
long before there was an official line.

"Unflinchingly and calmly, as steady and collected as if on
parade.... our 14 devoted Nursing Sisters faced the terrible
ordeal..." stated a CAMC survivor, Sergeant Knight. Gradually
survivors, who had witnessed the U-boat machine-gun the occupants revealed how the occupants of the 2 other lifeboats met
their fate, finally "The suction drew us quickly into the vacuum,
the boat tipped over and every occupant went under". It seemed
that Patzig was trying to cover-up his crime. There was no effort to
save anyone.

The final tally for the sinking of the Llandovery Castle was
the death of 14 Nursing Sisters, the CO, 5 Officers and 68 men
of the CAMC. Six men, including 1 Officer survived the sinking
and 3 were lucky enough to have stayed in Halifax.

REVENGE

We may never know what really happened on the Llandovery
Castle that night or whether it was carrying munitions. After the
War, two Officers of the U-86 were put on trial in Leipzig. The

Officer commanding, Patzig could not be found. It was established no one, who survived the War or was at the trial saw the lifeboats being fired at. Sergeant Knight's description of events was not even mentioned, indicating that it may of been fabricated for propaganda purposes. The 2 Officers, who did not witness any shooting, were imprisoned for 4 years.

What we do know is that there was a call for revenge, and there can be no doubt Canadian Troops extracted the revenge on German frontline troops on August 8th, 1918. In that classic memoir of the Great War, "Generals Die in Bed" by Charles Yale Harrison, a soldier in the 14th (Royal Montreal Regiment) Battalion describes the slaughter. An easier way to look at the event is to compare Prisoners captured by the Australians to those captured by the Canadians. Both Corps captured a similar amount of terrain, guns and machine-guns. However the Australians captured 8,000 Germans. The Canadians captured only 5,000!

THE TOUR OF MOREUIL WOOD

After Point 3 continue towards Roye on the D934. After 2.5 km the road intersects the D23, to Demuin and Moreuil. Turn right to Moreuil and after 1.0 km stop your car. The small wood to your left is Hollan Wood. Looking south-west, 1.5 km away is the modern Moreuil Wood. In 1918 the wood extended to the D23, where you now stand. The charge of Flowerdew's squadron took place across the open field in front of you.

The German offensive, launched from St. Quentin on March 21st, 1918 had driven the British 5th Army back so quickly that panic had taken hold. The retreat, by March 30th, 1918 was bordering on a rout. There seemed to be no way of stopping the Germans, who were now within 10 km of Amiens, a vital communications centre. Should Amiens fall the French and British Armies would be divided.

On March 30th the Germans were advancing across the ridge overlooking Moreuil (where you now stand) and infiltrating into the Wood. It seemed only a dramatic action would stem the German onslaught. The men of the Canadian Cavalry Brigade; Lord Strathcona's Horse, Royal Canadian Dragoons and Fort Garry

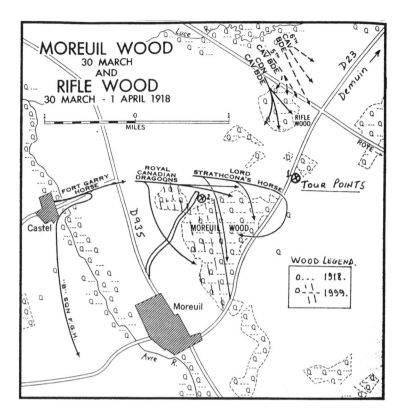

Horse were given orders to take the wood. Two squadrons of the
RCD (and later the FGH) attacked the south-west edge of the
wood, close to the village of Moreuil. The sudden appearance of
the calvary seemed to take the Germans by surprise and the troopers, dismounted, fought their way into the wood. The fighting was
often hand-to-hand but slowly the Canadians advanced to the
north-east corner of the wood where the fighting was continuous.

At the same time, two squadrons from the RCD and the LSH
tried to encircle the wood from the north. Mid-way along the
northern edge the Canadian cavalry entered the wood, and as in
the southern area, pushed the Germans back.

Between the two attacks 300 Germans were slowly being driven
out the eastern edge of the wood. "C" squadron of the Lord
Strathcona's Horse, under the command of Lieutenant Gordon
Flowerdew[13], circled the wood to the north and advanced along

---

[13] Gordon Muriel Flowerdew; born Billingford, England, January 2, 1885; died
Namps-au-Val, France, March 31, 1918.

THE CHARGE AT MOREUIL WOOD

J. B. Seely was a British adventurer and Member of Parliament. He had served with distinction in the Boer War. During the First World War he commanded the Canadian Cavalry Brigade. It was Seely who ordered the attack on Moreuil Wood. After the war he wrote a memoir, entitled "Adventure". This is how he described the battle:

"30th March, 1918. Then, with my aide-de-camp, an orderly with a little red pennant and my signal troop, I galloped down the hill, across the bridge over the Luce, through a field of young wheat and over a road to our front line. A few bullets flew about, but not many, for we were in dead ground, except to the enemy at the point of the wood.

"As I rode through our front line, who were lying down and firing, I said to a young captain: "We are going to retake the ridge. Fire on both sides of us, as close as you can, while the rest of us go up." He knelt up and shouted: "Good luck to you, sir." Our infantry opened a glorious fire on both sides of us as we galloped on. Five out of about twelve of my signal troop were shot by the enemy, but the remaining seven reached the wood, jumped off and opened fire. My orderly jammed the red flag into the ground at the point of the wood, and I looked back, to see my gallant brigade galloping forward by the way I had come. . . .

"Soon the brigade arrived. It is curious how galloping horses seem to magnify in power and number; it looked like a great host sweeping forward over the open country. I galloped up to Flowerdew, who commanded the leading squadron of Strathcona's, and as we rode along together I told him that his was the most adventurous task of all, but that I was confident he would succeed. With his gentle smile he turned to me and said, "I know, sir, I know, it is a splendid moment. I will try not to fail you."

"The Dragoons just ahead of us had suffered heavily and had failed to reach the north-east corner. But they had turned into the wood and engaged the enemy. The air was alive with bullets, but nobody minded a bit. It was strange to see the horses roll over like rabbits, and the men, when unwounded, jump up and run forward, sometimes catching the stirrups of their still mounted comrades.

"I went with Flowerdew to where we could see round the corner of the wood. He had lost comparatively few men up till then. He wheeled his four troops into line, and with a wild shout, a hundred yards in front of his men, charged down on the long thin column of Germans, marching into the wood.

"A short time later, when I arrived on the eastern face with the supporting squadron I found the survivors of this desperate charge securely ensconced in a little ditch, which bordered the wood, in twos and threes, each with a German machine-gun and with three or four Germans lying dead by their side. It was recorded that seventy Germans were killed by sword thrust alone outside the wood. I saw perhaps another two or three hundred lying there, who had been killed by machine-gun fire. In those brief moments we lost over eight hundred horses, but only three hundred men killed and wounded. The fanatical valour of my men on this strange day was equalled by the Bavarian defenders now surrounded in the wood. Hundreds of them were shot while they ran to their left to join their comrades still holding on to the south-east corner. Hundreds more stood their ground and were shot at point-blank range or were killed with the bayonet. Not one single man surrendered. As I rode through the wood on Warrior with the dismounted squadrons of Strathcona's I saw a handsome young Bavarian twenty yards in front of me miss an approaching Strathcona, and, as a consequence, receive a bayonet thrust right through the neck. He sank down with his back against a tree, the blood pouring from his throat. As I came close up to him I shouted out in German "Lie still, a stretcher-bearer will look after you." His eyes in his ashen-grey face seemed to blaze fire as he snatched up his rifle and fired his last shot at me, saying loudly: "Nein, nein. Ich will ungefangen sterben." Then he collapsed in a heap.

"After seeing the position at the eastern face of the wood I galloped back to my head-quarters, which Connolly had moved up to about a third of the way along the northern front."

the northern edge of the wood. They saw about 200 German troops roughly 200 metres to the east (100 metres west of where you are standing). Flowerdew had only two options; to retreat or to charge. He decided to charge. Across the open field (from the D23 to the modern Moreuil Wood) the Canadians galloped onto the Germans. The German machine-guns shot down many of the men and horses. Using their swords they hacked through two lines of German infantry, some even wheeled about and attacked the Germans again.

The charging Strathconas crossed the D23 (100 metres south of where you stand), wheeled and attacked the Germans in the north-east corner of the wood. The other Canadians in the wood joined them and together ousted the Germans. By 8:30 pm the Canadians were relieved. They had stemmed the German advance at Moreuil for at least another day.

Casualties among the Canadian Cavalry regiments were high. The RCD suffered 91 killed, wounded or missing. The Strathcona's had 37 killed and 120 wounded. Basically, 40% of the men involved in the battle were casualties. Amongst the wounded was Lieutenant Gordon Flowerdew whose courageous charge had saved the assault. Certainly if the Germans had been allowed to reinforce their men in the wood the day would have ended differently. Flowerdew, who was wounded in the thigh and hip early in the charge, made it into the wood, where he was evacuated to a dressing station at Namps-au-Val. He died the next day. For his courage, Gordon Flowerdew was awarded the Victoria Cross, posthumously.

The next day the depleted Canadian squadrons were used to drive the Germans from Rifle (or Dodo) Wood, 700 metres to the north-west of you.

To visit the village of Moreuil continue on the D23 into the village and turn right on the D935 and follow it for 1.3 km. After 1.3 km a small unnumbered road forks to your right, take it. It leads to the north-west corner of the wood. You can imagine the thundering hooves as the RCD galloped across your path. The road intersects the wood and you will pass through to what was, the northern edge. Straight ahead the LSH and RCD attacked the wood, and it was across your path that Flowerdew made his fateful charge.

Return to Moreuil and take the D23 back to the D934. Turn right to continue the tour of the Battle of Amiens.

The grave of Lieutenant Gordon Flowerdew, VC, of Lord Strathcona's Horse in Namps-au Val British Cemetery. Flowerdew died of wounds received in the epic charge at Moreuil Wood.

Namps-au Val is a small village, 18 km SW of Amiens, just south of the main road (N29) to Poix-de Picardie.

(PHOTO: NORM CHRISTIE)

No. 8 General Hospital. August 16th, 1918.

The following letter was sent to Mrs. David Thompson Christie from her son, John Christie. John, who had been wounded on August 14th at Parvillers, described the confused action east of the village. The action cost the life of his Company Commander, Vivian Drummond-Hay.

"Well I moved last night from the C.C.S. by Ambulance train to No. 8 General Hospital. We were very well looked after, everything nice to eat and drink, nothing to do all day only sleep. Had an X Ray photo taken and the bullet is lodged in my knee, and I go to Blighty tonight or tomorrow morning, and will be operated on there.

I don't feel any pain, unless I move and of course with a splint on I don't move very much.

On the way down here we passed a train of Soldiers going up to the front and I saw John Dickie, but he didn't see me. I am always wondering if Randall is home yet? Of course he is bound to be there, as he hasn't had a square meal for nine months [Randall was his younger brother, and my Grandfather, who had been wounded in the jaw by shrapnel, January 15th, 1918]. Thank Goodness my wound doesn't prevent me from eating. I hadn't had a meal for four days when I came down from the Line, nor a sleep for several days. Four of our Officers are in the Ward with me, all for Blighty except one. It was a pretty bad fix we were in for about two hours and it seems a miracle that we were not taken Prisoners or killed. We just started to move the Company back in time and the Fritz were all around us. We tried to get to close quarters with them, but couldn't as they were among the buildings and we were in the open fields. The Company Commander Major Drummond Hay was putting up a fight with a small party while I manoeuvred the rest of the Company back and I had just got over to him when a bullet hit one of the men, went right through his stomach and into my knee. It didn't knock me out and I was just going to speak to Drummond when he fell like a log and said "John I'm done" I tried to get him to his feet but he fell dead right in my arms, and we had to leave him. I carried on for about two hours, when I began to faint, however I got over it and walked to Battalion #2 and the Doctor made me get right out. Had a narrow escape before coming out, a Coal box landed between another Chap and I. He was shell shocked but it didn't bother me. It seems to be too good to be true. That I am so well out of it as it was one of the hardest days we have had for a long time. The Sun was terribly hot and our water was running short and we hadn't much to eat. But today the big attack has started again. I'll bet the Huns along that front were wishing they had never been born as our Staff are determined to get on and keep the Hun on the run."

John (sitting) and Randall Christie, Montreal 1919. Both wear wound stripes, and John, the ribbon of the Military Cross.

FOR FURTHER REFERENCE

The Battle of Amiens 1918 was the first of three great victories by the Canadian Corps in the last hundred days of the First World War. However the record of the Canadians was exceptional from their arrival in France in 1915 to the end of the war, and although this book has solely focused on one battle there is much more to know about the other Canadian battles. In addition to the Canadians, the Great War for Civilization has left many reminders of the sacrifice of British, French, Australian, New Zealander, South African, and German troops on the Western Front. There is much is worth seeing.

Below I have outlined a number of guidebooks which will assist in the understanding of, and visits to, the Great War battlefields on the Western Front. Of all the great battles in the Advance to Victory, Amiens was the one battle which has been most seriously addressed. The others battles have rarely been treated as much more than a continuation of the Battle of Amiens.

Battle Guides
Before Endeavours Fade, by R.E. Coombs. Battle of Britain Prints International, 1976.
The Somme Battlefields, by M. And M. Middlebrook. Viking 1981.
The Somme Then and Now, by J. Giles. Battle of Britain Prints , 1986.
The Western Front, Then and Now, by J. Giles. Battle of Britain Prints, 1992.
Australian Battlefields of the Western Front, by J. Laffin. Kangaroo Press, 1992.
The Canadians at Arras, by N.M. Christie. CEF BOOKS, 1997.
The Canadians at Cambrai, by N.M. Christie. CEF BOOKS, 1998.

The Battle of Amiens
The Official History of the Canadian Expeditionary Force 1914-19, by G.W.L. Nicholson. The Queen's Printer, 1962.
Canada's Hundred Days, by J.F.B. Livesay. Thomas Allen, 1919.
Spearhead to Victory, by D. Dancocks. Hurtig Publishers, 1987.
Only This, A War Retrospect, 1917-1918, by J.H. Pedley. CEF BOOKS, 1999.
Ghosts Have Warm Hands, by Will R. Bird. CEF BOOKS, 1997.